# FIRST 50 HYMNS

## YOU SHOULD PLAY ON THE PIANO


2 ..... Abide with Me
6 ..... All Creatures of Our God and King
8 ..... All Hail the Power of Jesus' Name
3 ..... Amazing Grace
10 ..... America, the Beautiful
13 ..... Battle Hymn of the Republic
16 ..... Be Thou My Vision
20 ..... Beautiful Savior
22 ..... Blessed Assurance
17 ..... Come, Christians, Join to Sing
24 ..... Come, Thou Almighty King
26 ..... Come, Thou Fount of Every Blessing
28 ..... Come, Ye Thankful People, Come
30 ..... Crown Him with Many Crowns
32 ..... Eternal Father, Strong to Save
31 ..... For the Beauty of the Earth
34 ..... Have Thine Own Way, Lord
36 ..... Holy, Holy, Holy
38 ..... How Firm a Foundation
40 ..... I Am Thine, O Lord
42 ..... I Love to Tell the Story
46 ..... I Need Thee Every Hour
48 ..... I Sing the Mighty Power of God
50 ..... I Surrender All
52 ..... Immortal, Invisible
54 ..... It Is Well with My Soul
37 ..... Jesus Loves Me
56 ..... Jesus Paid It All
58 ..... Jesus Shall Reign
60 ..... Joyful, Joyful, We Adore Thee
62 ..... Leaning on the Everlasting Arms
64 ..... A Mighty Fortress Is Our God
66 ..... My Faith Looks Up to Thee
57 ..... Nearer, My God, to Thee
68 ..... O for a Thousand Tongues to Sing
70 ..... O Master, Let Me Walk with Thee
72 ..... O Worship the King
69 ..... Praise God, from Whom All Blessings Flow
74 ..... Praise to the Lord, the Almighty
76 ..... Rock of Ages
80 ..... Savior, Like a Shepherd Lead Us
77 ..... Softly and Tenderly
82 ..... This Is My Father's World
84 ..... 'Tis So Sweet to Trust in Jesus
86 ..... We Gather Together
88 ..... Were You There?
90 ..... What a Friend We Have in Jesus
96 ..... When I Survey the Wondrous Cross
92 ..... Whiter than Snow
94 ..... Wondrous Love


T0039458

ISBN 978-1-5400-2602-6

HAL•LEONARD®

For all works contained herein:
Unauthorized copying, arranging, adapting, recording, Internet posting, public performance, or other distribution of the music in this publication is an infringement of copyright.
Infringers are liable under the law.

Visit Hal Leonard Online at
**www.halleonard.com**

Contact Us:
**Hal Leonard**
7777 West Bluemound Road
Milwaukee, WI 53213
Email: info@halleonard.com

In Europe contact:
**Hal Leonard Europe Limited**
Distribution Centre, Newmarket Road
Bury St Edmunds, Suffolk, IP33 3YB
Email: info@halleonardeurope.com

In Australia contact:
**Hal Leonard Australia Pty. Ltd.**
4 Lentara Court
Cheltenham, Victoria, 3192 Australia
Email: info@halleonard.com.au

# ABIDE WITH ME

Words by HENRY F. LYTE
Music by WILLIAM H. MONK

Copyright © 2018 by HAL LEONARD LLC
International Copyright Secured All Rights Reserved

# AMAZING GRACE

Words by JOHN NEWTON
From *A Collection of Sacred Ballads*
Traditional American Melody
From Carrell and Clayton's *Virginia Harmony*

Copyright © 1995 by HAL LEONARD CORPORATION
International Copyright Secured All Rights Reserved

G G7 C
I once was lost, but now am
'Tis grace has brought me safe thus
Gsus G Em G/D D7 G C/G
found, was blind, but now I see.
far, and grace will lead me home.
G G7 C
'Twas grace that taught my heart to
The Lord has prom - ised good to
G
fear and grace my fears re -
me, His word my hope se -

D G G7
lieved. How pre - cious did that
cures. He will my shield and
C Gsus G Em G/D D7
grace ap - pear the hour I first be -
por - tion be as long as life en -
1.
G C/G G
Both hands 8va
C/E Cm/E♭ D7
lieved.
G D
(8va)
Through
2.
C G
dures.
molto rit.

# ALL CREATURES OF OUR GOD AND KING

Words by FRANCIS OF ASSISI
Translated by WILLIAM HENRY DRAPER
Music from *Geistliche Kirchengesang*

Copyright © 2018 by HAL LEONARD LLC
International Copyright Secured All Rights Reserved

F Bb/D Csus C F/A
burn - ing sun with gold - en beam, Thou
ris - ing morn, in praise re - joice; Ye
fire so mas - ter - ful and bright, that
F Bb/D F Bb/D Csus/Bb F/A Gm F/A
sil - ver moon with soft - er gleam,
lights of eve - ning, find a voice!
giv - est man both warmth and light,
O ___ praise Him! O ___
Csus/Bb C Dm C/E F G C Dm C/E F Gm C/E D/F# Gm F/A
praise Him! Al - le - lu - ia! Al - le - lu - ia! Al - le -
Bb6 C7
lu -
1., 2.
F
ia!
Thou
Thou
3.
F
ia!

# ALL HAIL THE POWER OF JESUS' NAME

Words by EDWARD PERRONET
Altered by JOHN RIPPON
Music by OLIVER HOLDEN

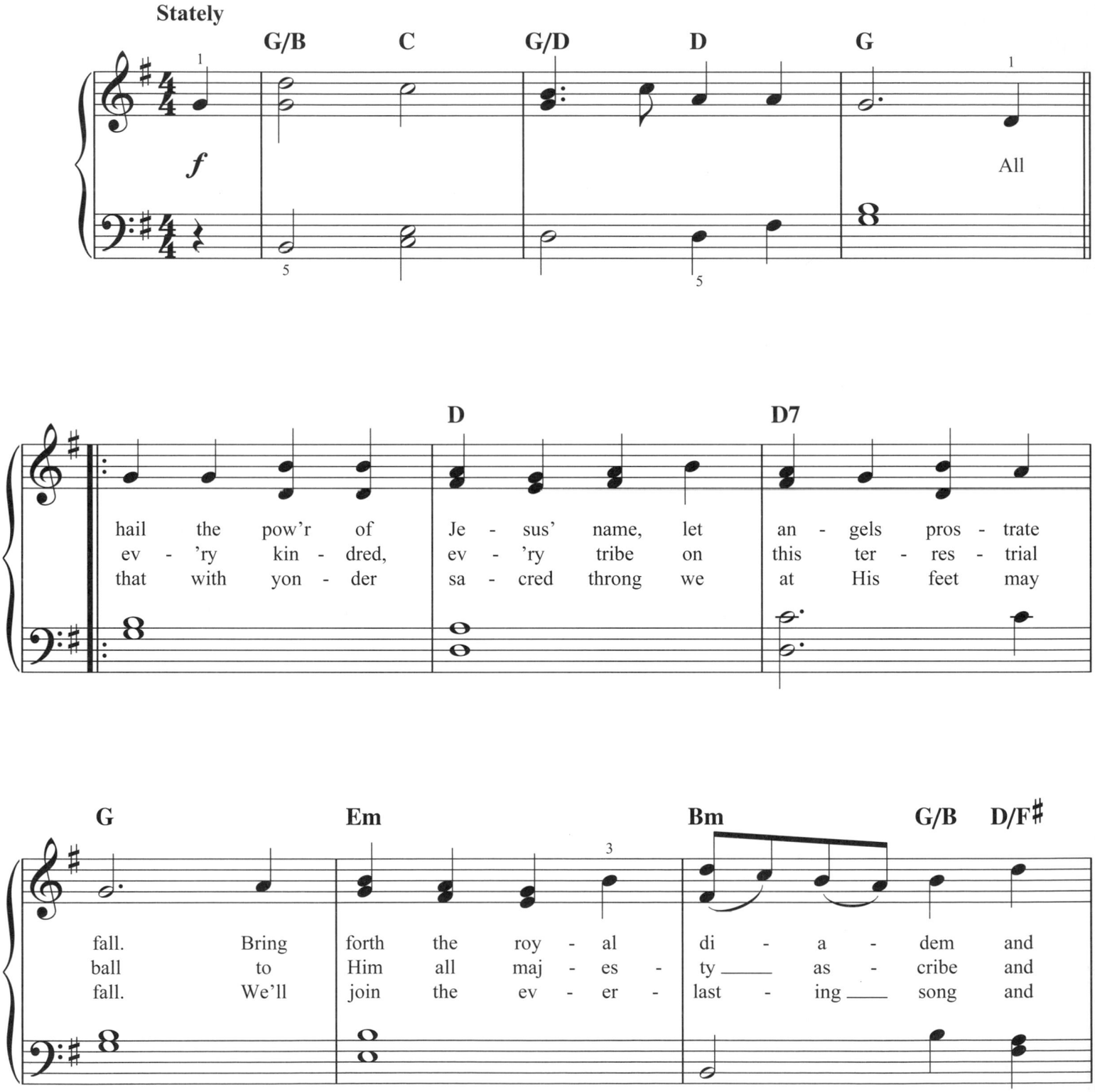


Copyright © 2018 by HAL LEONARD LLC
International Copyright Secured All Rights Reserved

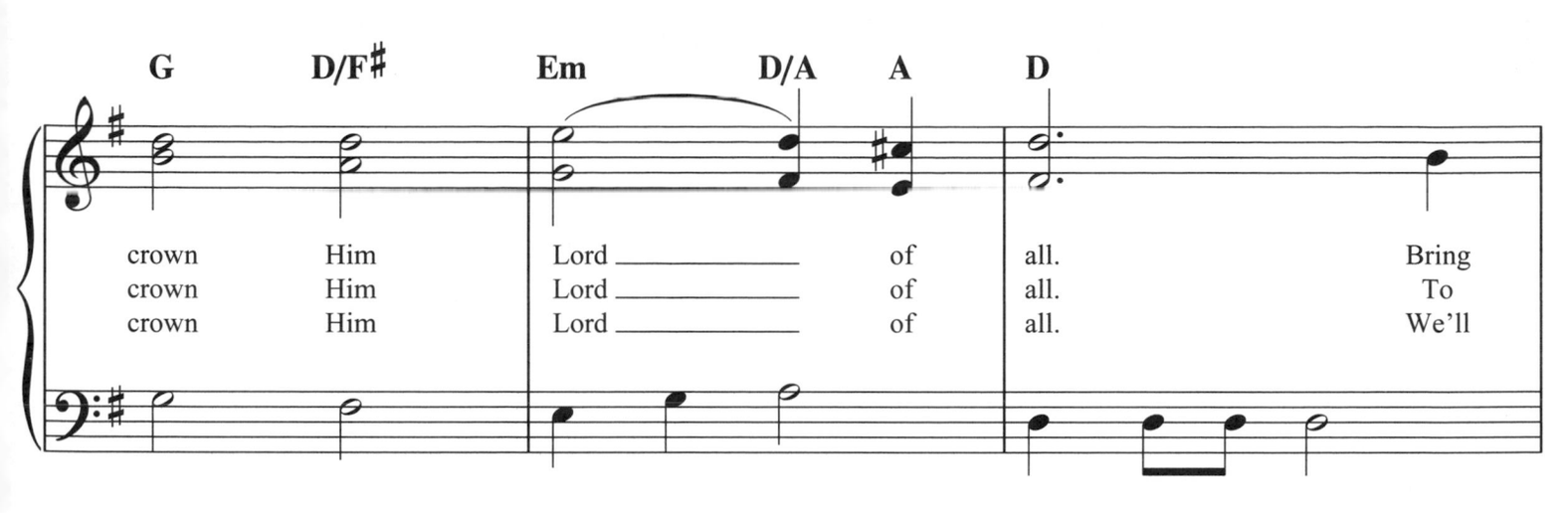
G D/F♯ Em D/A A D
crown Him Lord of all. Bring
crown Him Lord of all. To
crown Him Lord of all. We'll

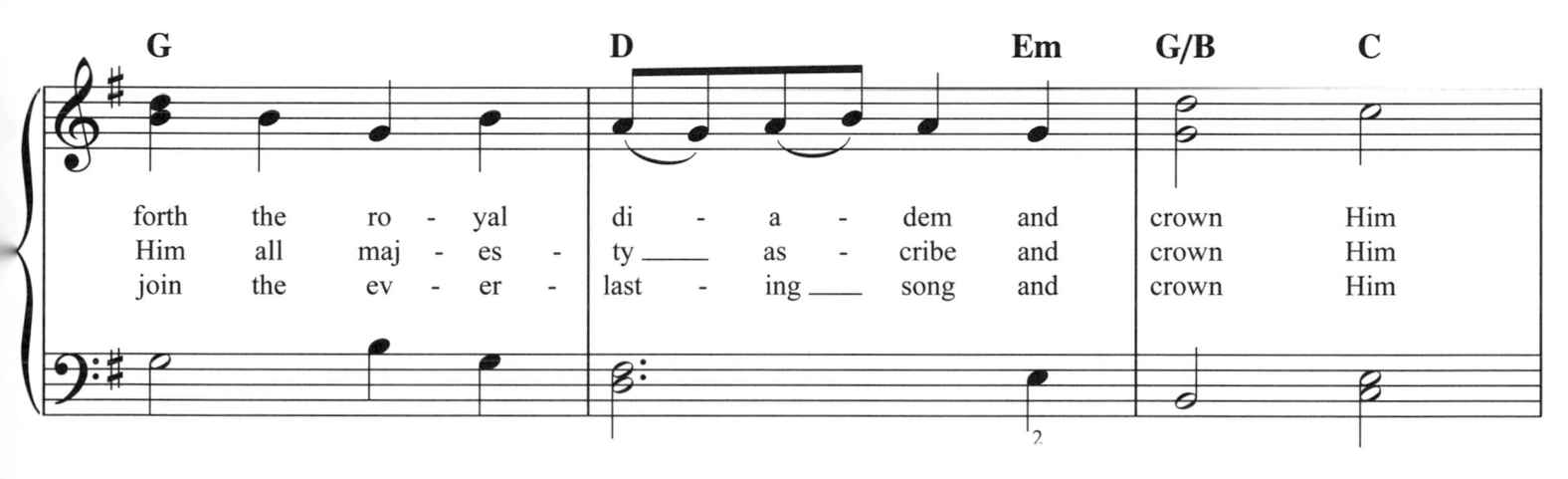
G D Em G/B C
forth the ro - yal di - a - dem and crown Him
Him all maj - es - ty as - cribe and crown Him
join the ev - er - last - ing song and crown Him
2

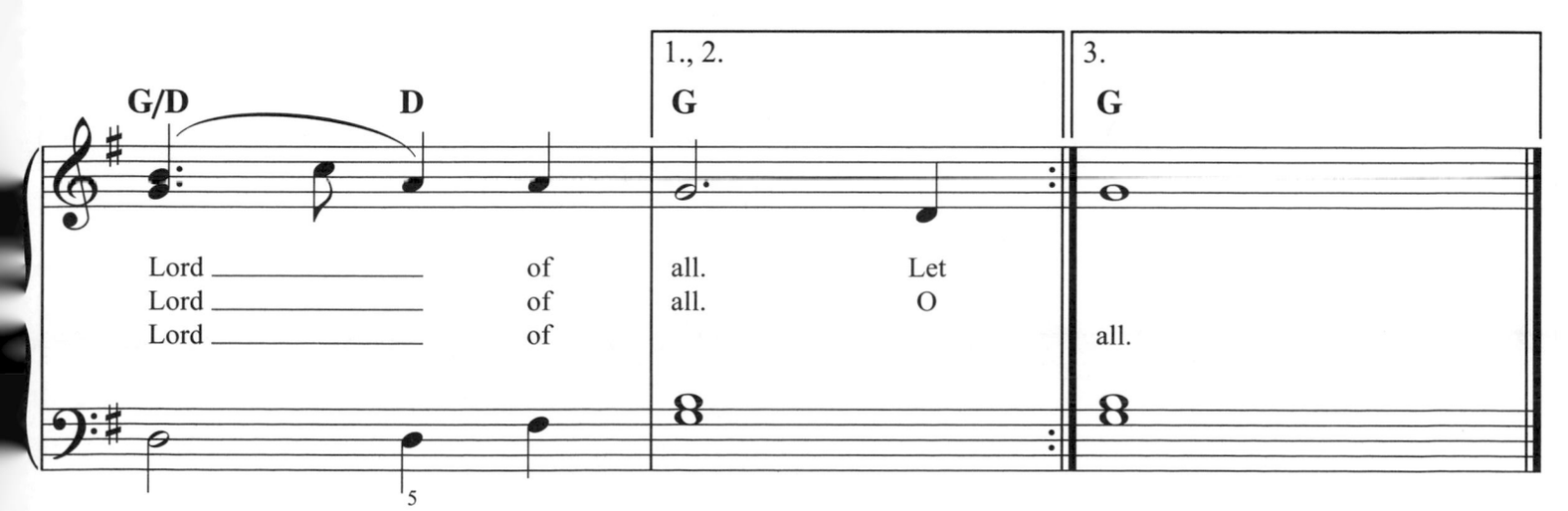
G/D D
1., 2.
G
3.
G
Lord of all. Let
Lord of all. O
Lord of all.
5

# AMERICA, THE BEAUTIFUL

Words by KATHARINE LEE BATES
Music by SAMUEL A. WARD

Copyright © 2018 by HAL LEONARD LLC
International Copyright Secured All Rights Reserved

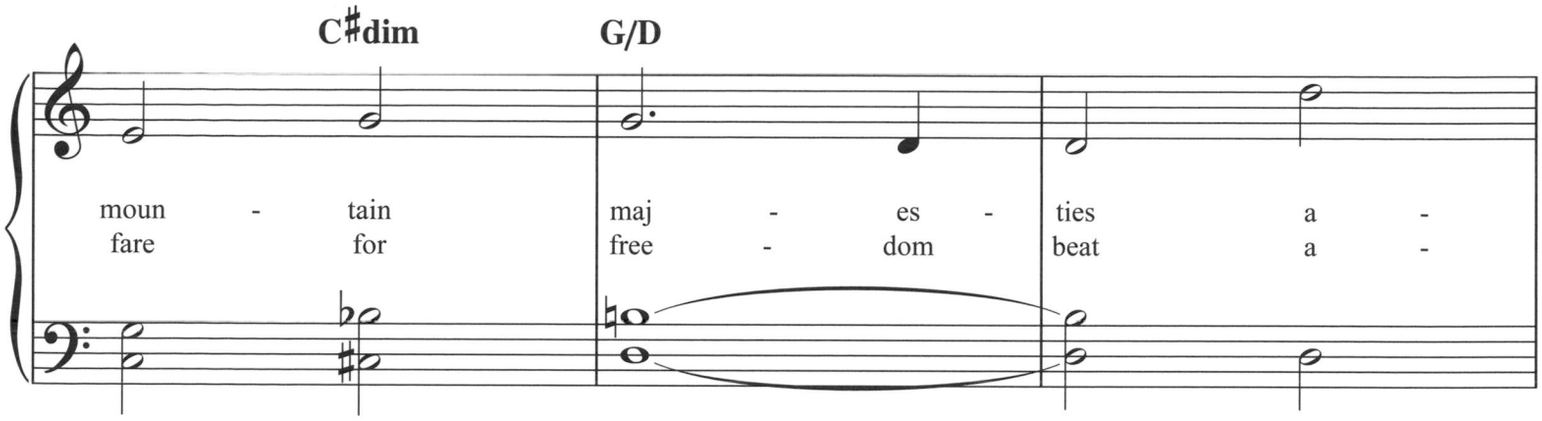
C♯dim
G/D
moun - tain maj - es - ties a -
fare for free - dom beat a -

G
D7/F♯
G
bove the fruit - ed plain! ___
cross the wil - der - ness! ___

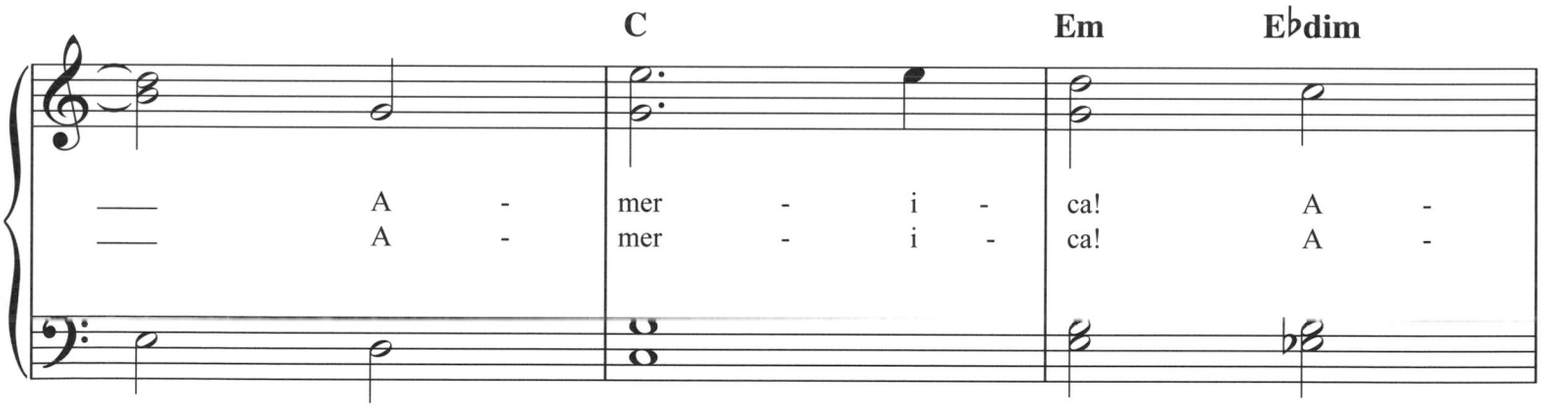
C
Em
E♭dim
___ A - mer - i - ca! A -
___ A - mer - i - ca! A -

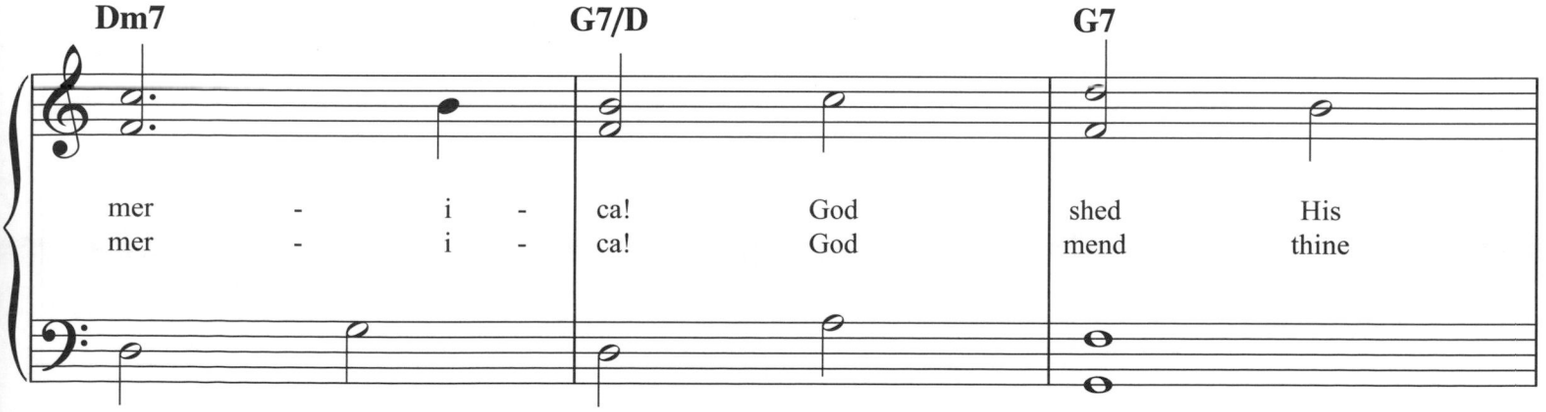
Dm7
G7/D
G7
mer - i - ca! God shed His
mer - i - ca! God mend thine

F/A G/B C
grace on thee, and
ev - 'ry flaw, con -
F F♯dim C/G
crown thy good with broth - er -
firm thy soul in self - con -
C F Dm7 G7
hood, from sea to shin - ing
trol, Thy lib - er - ty in
1.
C Dm G7
sea. O
2.
C F/A C
law.
rit.

# BATTLE HYMN OF THE REPUBLIC

Words by JULIA WARD HOWE
Music by WILLIAM STEFFE

Copyright © 2018 by HAL LEONARD LLC
International Copyright Secured All Rights Reserved

C/G
C
grapes of wrath are stored. He hath loos'd the fate - ful
eve - ning dews and damps. I have read his right - eous
Am
light - ning of His ter - ri - ble swift sword. His
sen - tence by the dim and flar - ing lamps. His
Dm
G7sus
G7
C
truth is march - ing on.
day is march - ing on.
C/G
2
Glo - ry, glo - ry, hal - le - lu -

F
jah!
Glo - ry, glo - ry, hal - le -
C/G
C
lu - jah!
Glo - ry, glo - ry, hal - le -
E/G♯
Am
Dm/F
C/G
G7
lu - jah! His truth is march - ing
f
1.
C
on. I have
2.
C
on.
rit.

# BE THOU MY VISION

Traditional Irish
Translated by MARY E. BYRNE

Copyright © 2018 by HAL LEONARD LLC
International Copyright Secured All Rights Reserved

# COME, CHRISTIANS, JOIN TO SING

Words by CHRISTIAN HENRY BATEMAN
Traditional Spanish Melody

Copyright © 2018 by HAL LEONARD LLC
International Copyright Secured All Rights Reserved

C/G Bm/F♯ Am/E D7 G Am/E E7/G♯ Am G D7
heart and voice be - fore His throne re - joice;
guide and friend; to us He'll con - de - scend;
2
G Em Cmaj7 D G Am
praise is His gra - cious choice: Al - le - lu - ia!
His love shall nev - er end: Al - le - lu - ia!
1.
C/D D7 G
A - men!
2.
C/D D7 G
A - men!
C C+
Praise yet our
F/C Cmaj7 C Fm C/E G7 C
Christ a - gain: Al - le - lu - ia! A - men!

C+ F/C Cmaj7 C Fm C/E G7 C
Life shall not end the strain; Al - le - lu - ia! A - men!
Dm7/C Em/B F/A Em/B Dm7/C C Dm7/C Em/B
On heav - en's bliss - ful shore His good - ness
F/A Em/B Dm7/C C F Cmaj7
we'll a - dore, sing - ing for - ev - er - more:
C Fm/C C/E G7 Am B♭7 C
"Al - le - lu - ia! A - men!"
rit.

# BEAUTIFUL SAVIOR

Words from *Munsterisch Gesangbuch*
Translated by JOSEPH A. SEISS
Music adapted from Silesian Folk Tune

Copyright © 2018 by HAL LEONARD LLC
International Copyright Secured All Rights Reserved

G D7/A G Dsus D
God and Son of Man!
flow'rs of bloom - ing spring:
G/B C G/D E7 Am E7/B Am/C
Tru - ly I'd love Thee, tru - ly I'd
Je - sus is fair - er, Je - sus is
D7 G G/B C
serve Thee, light of my soul, my
pur - er; He makes our sor - r'wing
G/D D7 1. G 2. G
joy, my crown.
spir - it sing.

# BLESSED ASSURANCE

Lyrics by FANNY J. CROSBY
Music by PHOEBE PALMER KNAPP

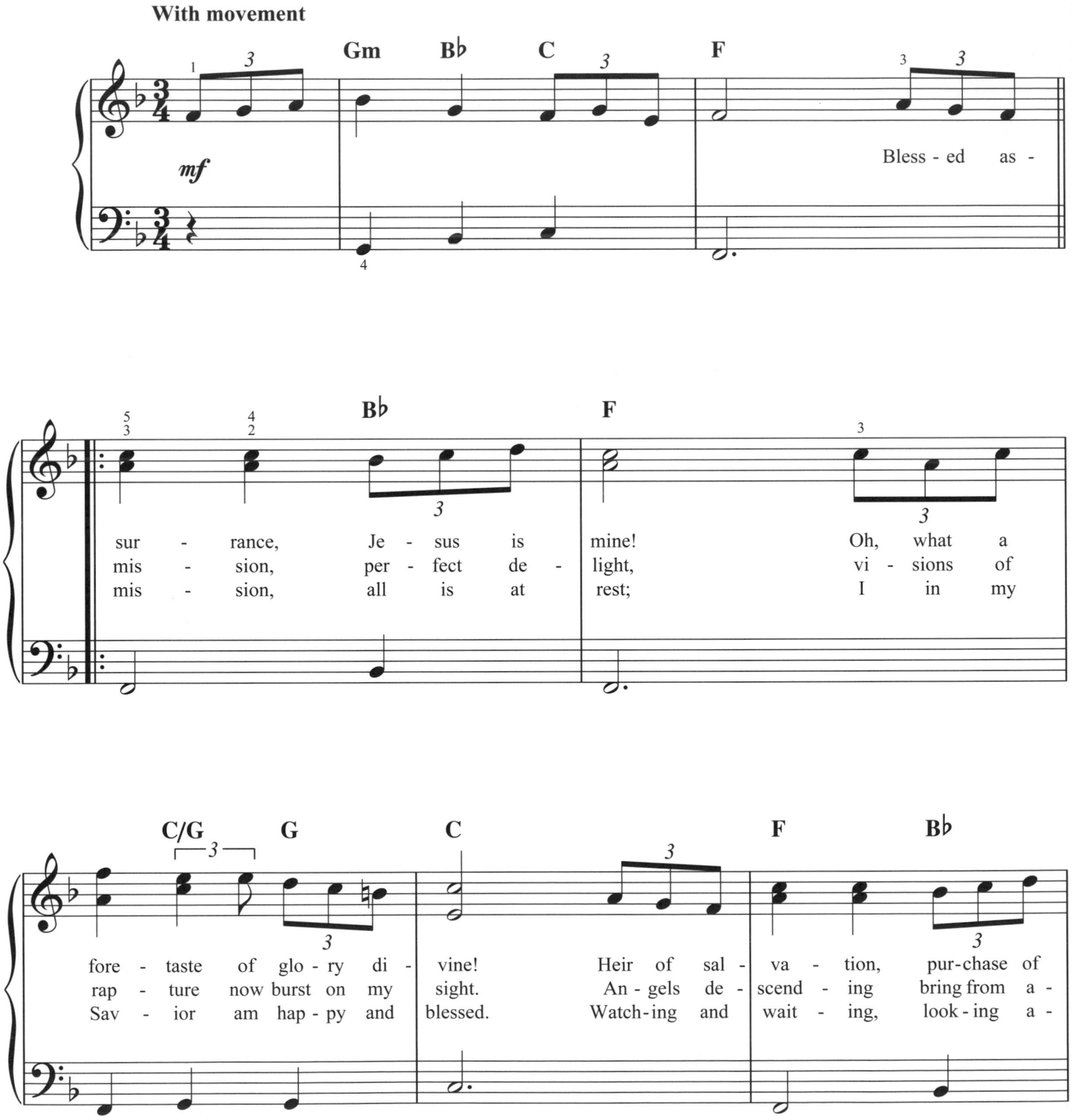


Copyright © 2018 by HAL LEONARD LLC
International Copyright Secured All Rights Reserved

F Gm B♭ C F C
God, born of His Spir - it, washed in His blood.
bove ech - oes of mer - cy, whis - pers of love.
bove, filled with His good - ness, lost in His love.
This is my
F B♭ F B♭ F/A C/G
sto - ry, this is my song, prais - ing my Sav - ior all the day
C F B♭ F
long. This is my sto - ry, this is my song, prais - ing my
Gm B♭ C
Sav - ior all the day
1., 2.
F
long. Per - fect sub -
3.
F
long.

# COME, THOU ALMIGHTY KING

Traditional
Music by FELICE DE GIARDINI

Copyright © 2018 by HAL LEONARD LLC
International Copyright Secured All Rights Reserved

Am G D/F♯ G
Come, Ho - ly Com - for - ter, Thy sa - cred
Thrice ho - ly Three ___ in One, on earth Thy
D7 G D G Bm
wit - ness bear in this glad hour:
will ___ be done from shore to shore.
D7 G D7 G
Thou who al - might - y art, rule now in ev - 'ry heart,
Thy sov - 'reign maj - es - ty may we in glo - ry see,
G/D G/B Am/C G/D D7
and ne'er from us de - part, Spir - it of pow'r.
and to e - ter - ni - ty love and a - dore.
1. G
2. G

# COME, THOU FOUNT OF EVERY BLESSING

Words by ROBERT ROBINSON
Music from JOHN WYETH's *Repository of Sacred Music*

Copyright © 2018 by HAL LEONARD LLC
International Copyright Secured All Rights Reserved

D C G D G
ceas - ing, call for songs of loud - est praise. Teach me ___
bring me safe - ly home by Thy good grace. Je - sus ___
fet - ter, bind my wan - d'ring heart to Thee. Prone to ___
Bm C C/G G G Bm C
some mel - o - dious son - net, sung by ___ flam - ing tongues a -
sought me when a stran - ger, wan - d'ring from the fold of
wan - der, Lord, I feel ___ it, prone to ___ leave the God I
G D G/D
bove. Praise His name, I'm fixed up - on it, name of
God. He, to res - cue me from dan - ger, bought me
love. Here's my heart, O take and seal it; seal it
1., 2. 3.
C G D G G
God's re - deem - ing love. Hith - er -
with His pre - cious blood. O to
for Thy courts a - bove.

# COME, YE THANKFUL PEOPLE, COME

Words by HENRY ALFORD
Music by GEORGE JOB ELVEY

Copyright © 2018 by HAL LEONARD LLC
International Copyright Secured All Rights Reserved

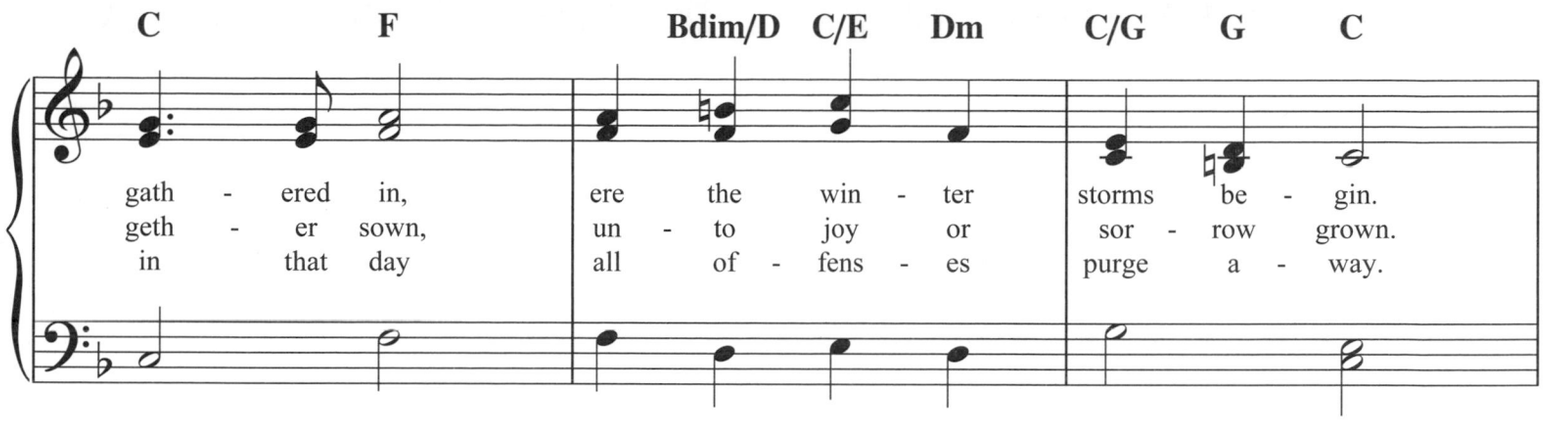
C F Bdim/D C/E Dm C/G G C
gath - ered in, ere the win - ter storms be - gin.
geth - er sown, un - to joy or sor - row grown.
in that day all of - fens - es purge a - way.

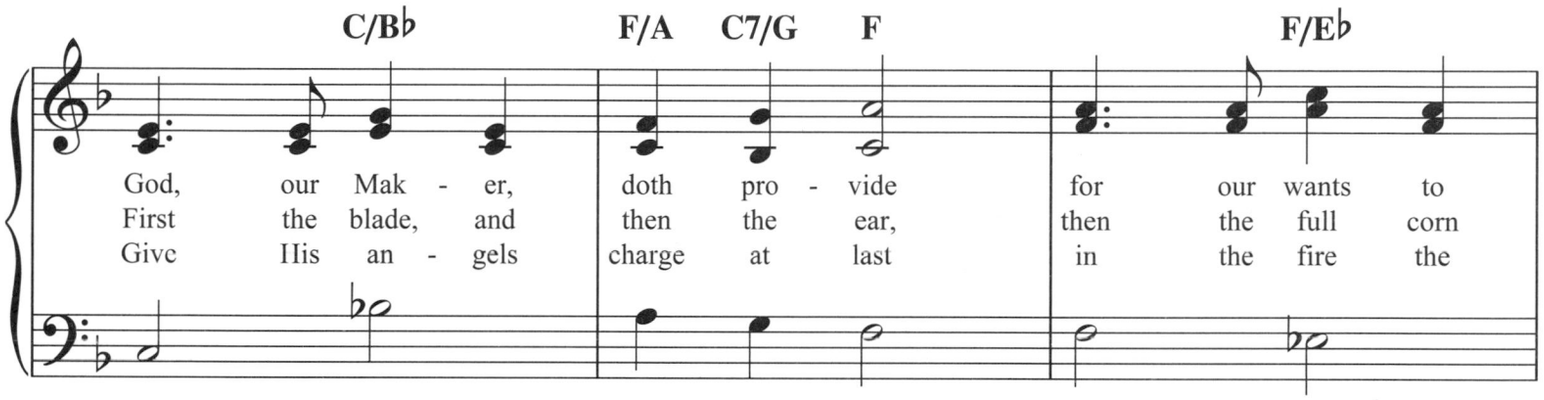
C/B♭ F/A C7/G F F/E♭
God, our Mak - er, doth pro - vide for our wants to
First the blade, and then the ear, then the full corn
Give His an - gels charge at last in the fire the

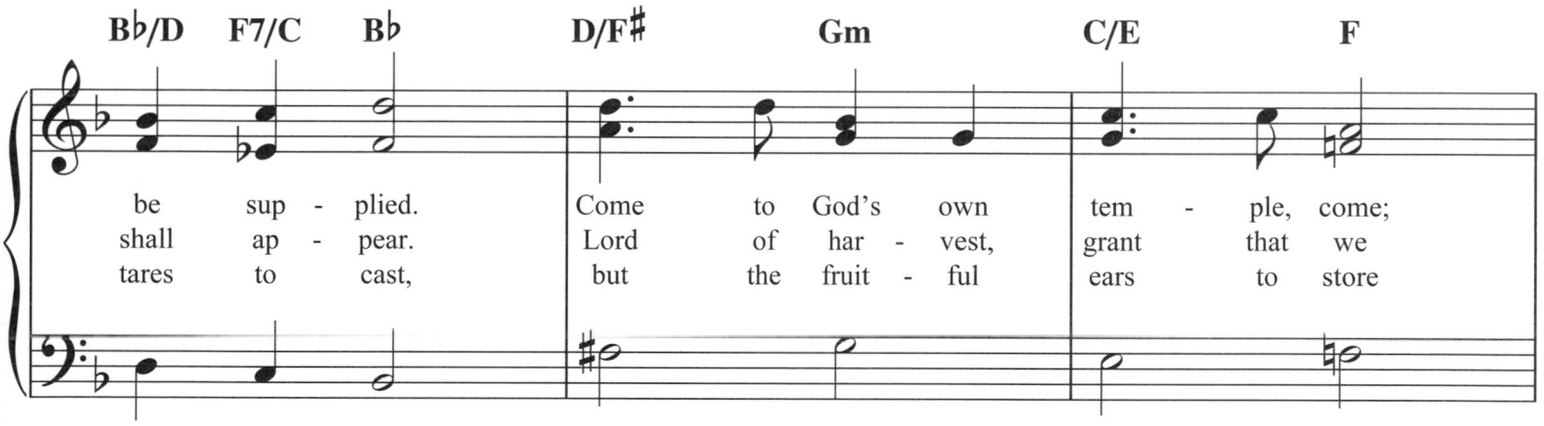
B♭/D F7/C B♭ D/F♯ Gm C/E F
be sup - plied. Come to God's own tem - ple, come;
shall ap - pear. Lord of har - vest, grant that we
tares to cast, but the fruit - ful ears to store

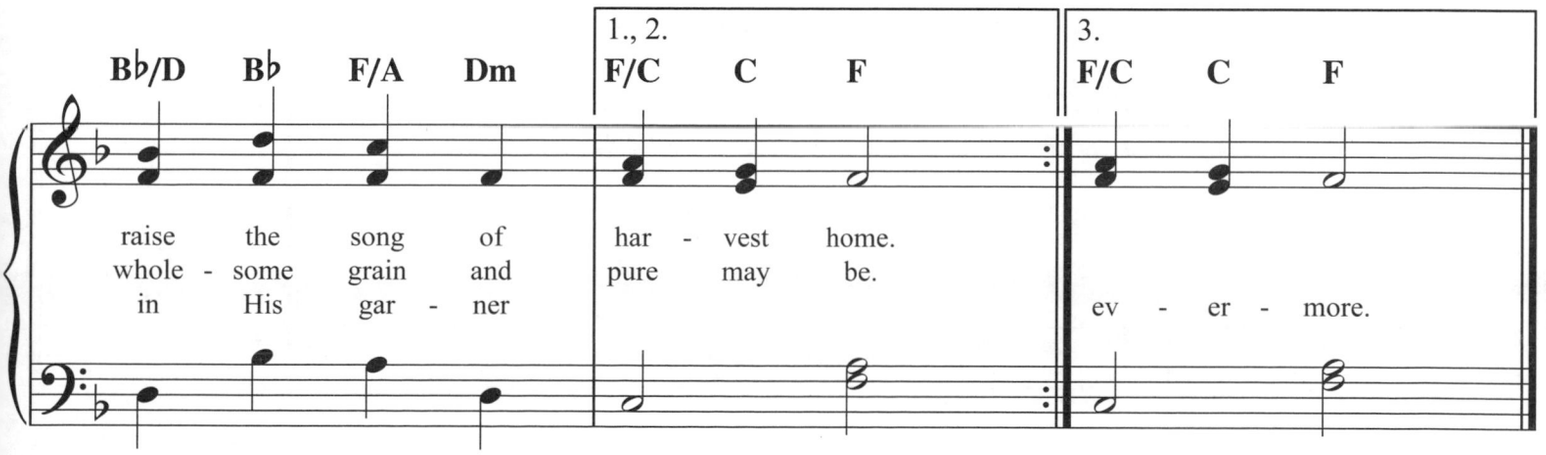
B♭/D B♭ F/A Dm
1., 2.
F/C C F
3.
F/C C F
raise the song of har - vest home.
whole - some grain and pure may be.
in His gar - ner ev - er - more.

# CROWN HIM WITH MANY CROWNS

Words by MATTHEW BRIDGES
and GODFREY THRING
Music by GEORGE JOB ELVEY

Copyright © 2014 by HAL LEONARD CORPORATION
International Copyright Secured All Rights Reserved

# FOR THE BEAUTY OF THE EARTH

Words by FOLLIOT S. PIERPOINT
Music by CONRAD KOCHER

Copyright © 2014 by HAL LEONARD CORPORATION
International Copyright Secured All Rights Reserved

# ETERNAL FATHER, STRONG TO SAVE

Words by WILLIAM WHITING
Music by JOHN BACCHUS DYKES

Copyright © 2018 by HAL LEONARD LLC
International Copyright Secured All Rights Reserved

C C/E F C G/B Am D G
sa - cred Spir - it, who did brood up - on the wa - ters
Trin - i - ty of love and pow'r, our breth - ren shield is
D G C A7 D B/D♯
dark and rude, who bid their an - gry tu - mult cease, and
dan - ger's hour, from rock and tem - pest, fire and foe, pro -
Em B7/F♯ Em/G Am Em/B B Em C7 F
gav - est light and life and peace: O hear us when we
tect them where - so - o'er they go. Thus ev - er - more shall
D7 G G7 C Dm/F C/G
cry to Thee for those in per - il
rise to Thee glad hymns of praise from
1.
G7/F C/E
on the sea. O
2.
G7/F C
land and sea.

# HAVE THINE OWN WAY, LORD

Words by ADELAIDE A. POLLARD
Music by GEORGE C. STEBBINS

Copyright © 2018 by HAL LEONARD LLC
International Copyright Secured All Rights Reserved

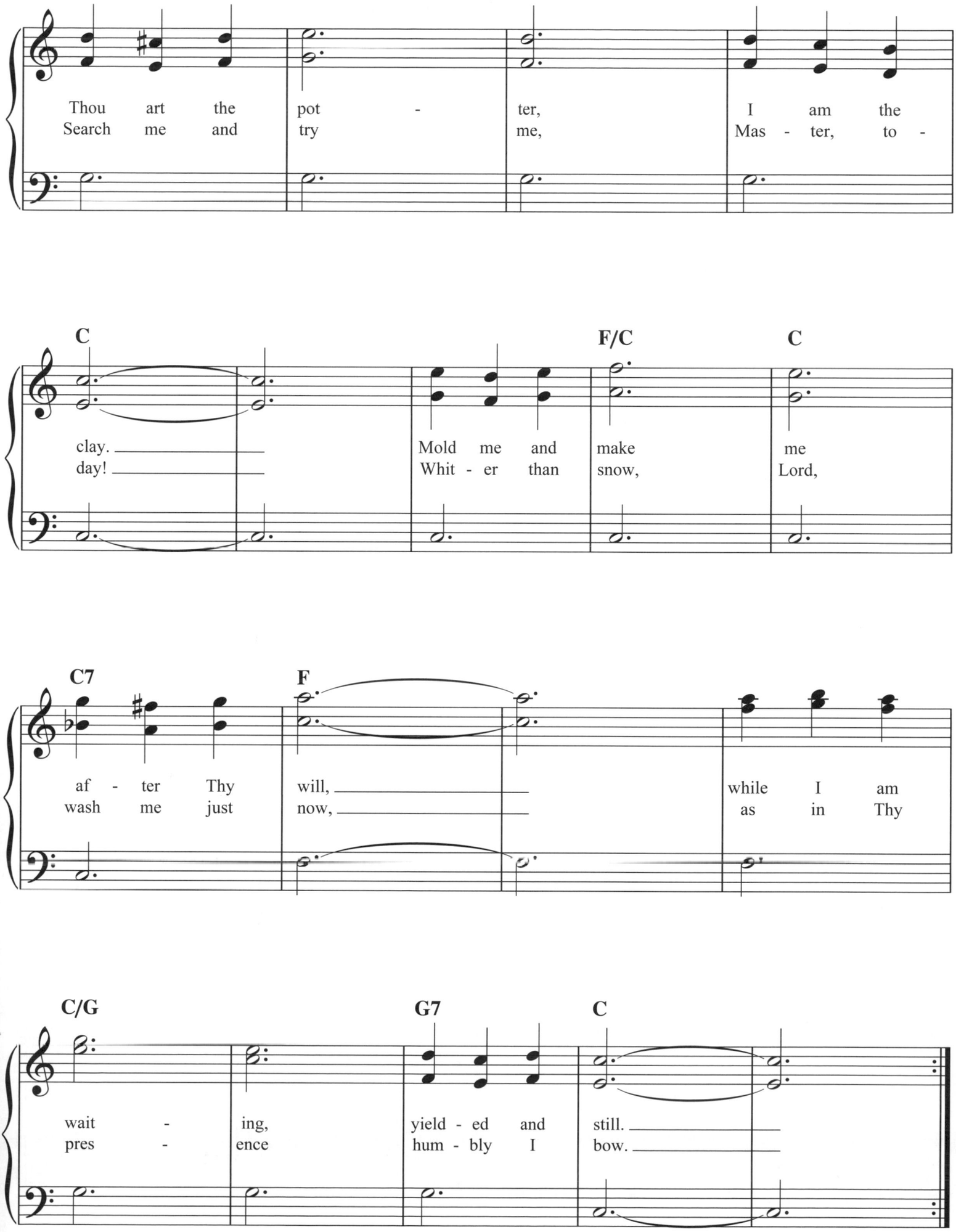
Thou art the pot - ter, I am the
Search me and try me, Mas - ter, to -
C
F/C
C
clay.
day!
Mold me and make me
Whit - er than snow, Lord,
C7
F
af - ter Thy will,
wash me just now,
while I am
as in Thy
C/G
G7
C
wait - ing, yield - ed and still.
pres - ence hum - bly I bow.

# HOLY, HOLY, HOLY

Text by REGINALD HEBER
Music by JOHN B. DYKES

Copyright © 2018 by HAL LEONARD LLC
International Copyright Secured All Rights Reserved

# JESUS LOVES ME

Words by ANNA B. WARNER
Music by WILLIAM B. BRADBURY

Copyright © 1993 by HAL LEONARD CORPORATION
International Copyright Secured All Rights Reserved

# HOW FIRM A FOUNDATION

Words from JOHN RIPPON'S *A Selection of Hymns*
Early American Melody

Copyright © 2018 by HAL LEONARD LLC
International Copyright Secured All Rights Reserved

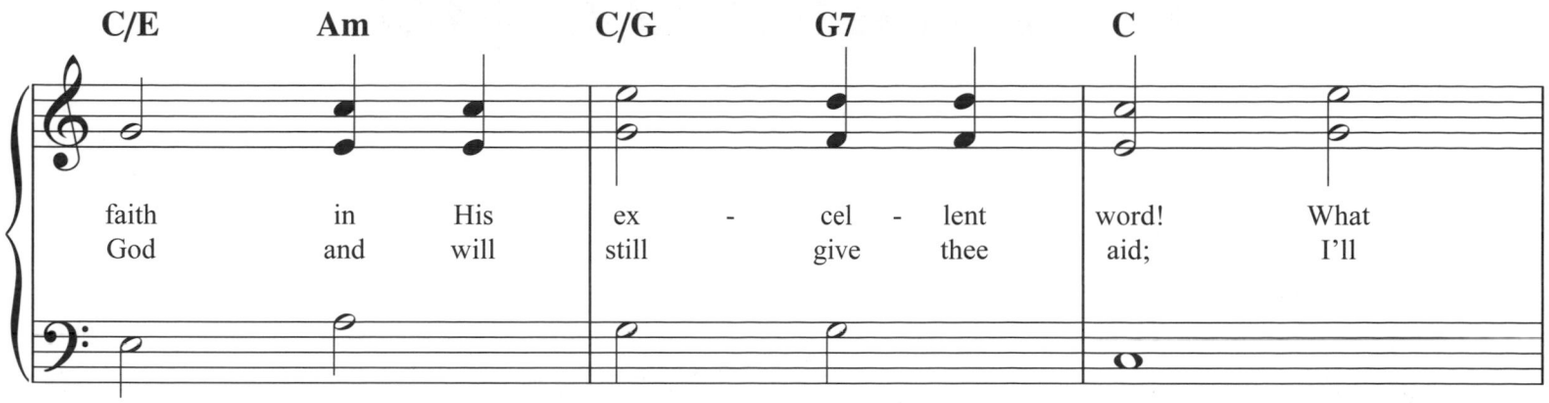
C/E Am C/G G7 C
faith in His ex - cel - lent word! What
God and will still give thee aid; I'll

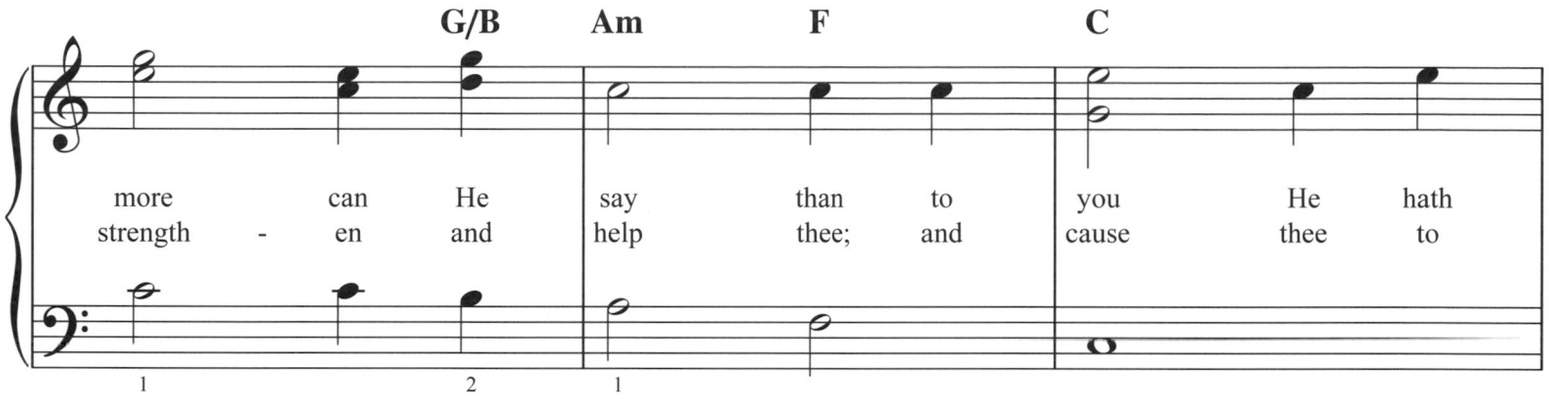
G/B Am F C
more can He say than to you He hath
strength - en and help thee; and cause thee to
1 2 1

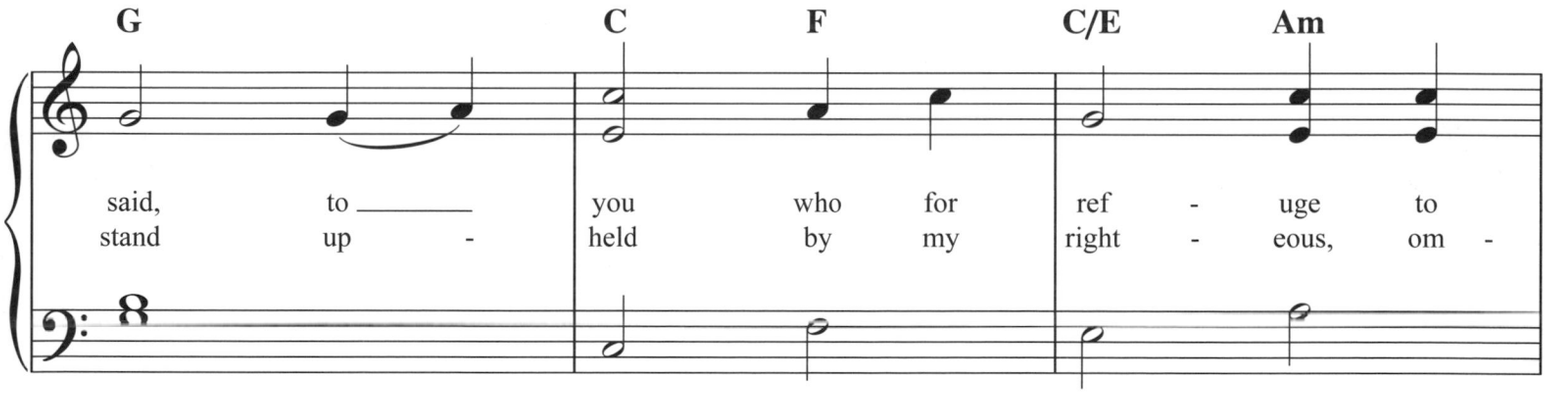
G C F C/E Am
said, to _____ you who for ref - uge to
stand up - held by my right - eous, om -

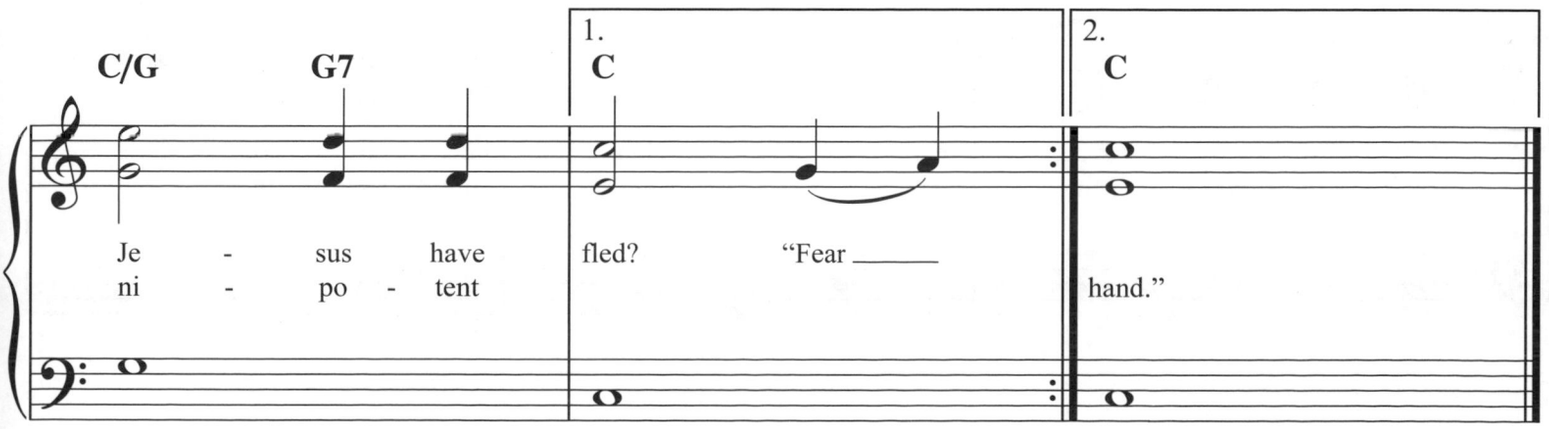
C/G G7 1. C 2. C
Je - sus have fled? "Fear _____
ni - po - tent hand."

# I AM THINE, O LORD

Words by FANNY J. CROSBY
Music by WILLIAM H. DOANE

Copyright © 2018 by HAL LEONARD LLC
International Copyright Secured All Rights Reserved

G C Am D D7 G
3
arms of faith and be clos - er drawn to Thee.
stead - fast hope, and my will be lost in Thine.
Draw me
C G G/B C G/B Am G
near - er, near - er, bless - ed Lord, to the cross where Thou hast
D G D/A G/B G7/B C
died; draw me near - er, near - er, near - er, bless - ed Lord, to Thy
G/D
pre - cious, bleed - ing
1.
G
side. Con - se -
2.
G
side.

# I LOVE TO TELL THE STORY

Words by A. CATHERINE HANKEY
Music by WILLIAM G. FISCHER

Copyright © 2018 by HAL LEONARD LLC
International Copyright Secured All Rights Reserved

F Dm B♭7
love to tell the sto - ry be - cause I know 'tis ____
love to tell the sto - ry, for some have nev - er ____
A B♭ Bdim F/C Dm
true; it sat - is - fies my long - ings as
heard the mes - sage of sal - va - tion from
Gm C7 F C7
noth - ing else can do.
God's own ho - ly word.
I love to tell the
F F7 B♭ E♭7 F
sto - ry 'twill be my theme in glo - ry to

F/A F7/E♭ B♭ Bdim F/C Dm Gm C7
tell the old, old sto - ry of Je - sus and His
1. F
love. I
2. F
love. I love to tell the
B♭ F/A
sto - ry; for those who know it best seem
C7 A7/C♯ Dm Am G7 D♭7 C7
hun - ger - ing and thirst - ing to hear it, like the rest. And

F A/E Dm B♭(♭5) A
when, in scenes of glo - ry, I sing the new, new _ song, 'twill
B♭ Bdim F/C Gm C7 F
be the old, old sto - ry that I have loved so long. I
C7 F B7♭5 B♭maj7 E♭7 F
love to tell the sto - ry, 'twill be my theme in glo - ry to
F7/E♭ B♭ Bdim F/C Dm Gm C7 F B♭ F
tell the old, _ old sto - ry of Je - sus and His love.

# I NEED THEE EVERY HOUR

Words by ANNIE S. HAWKS
Music by ROBERT LOWRY

Copyright © 2014 by HAL LEONARD CORPORATION
International Copyright Secured All Rights Reserved

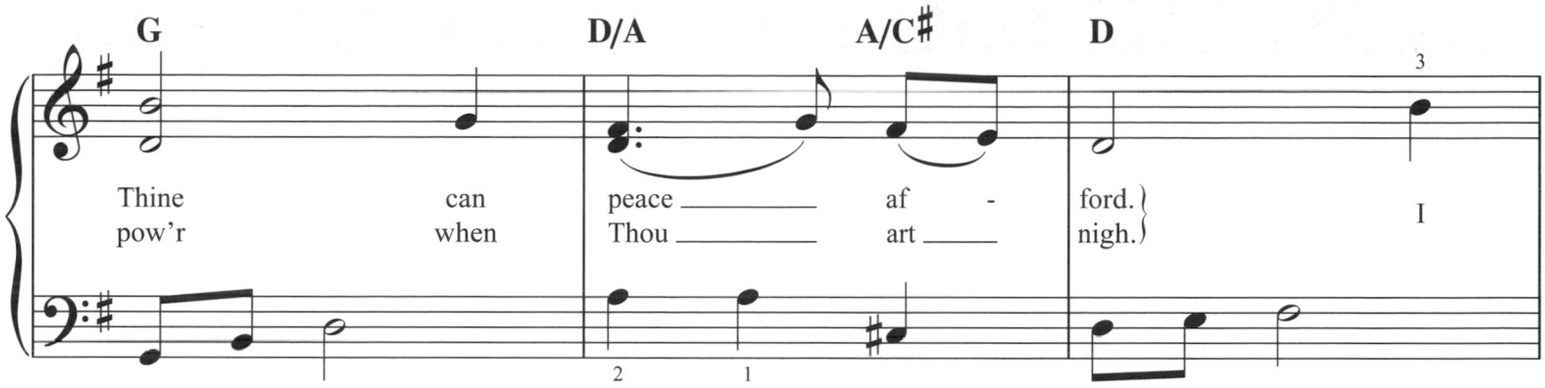
G
D/A
A/C♯
D
Thine can peace af - ford.
pow'r when Thou art nigh.
I

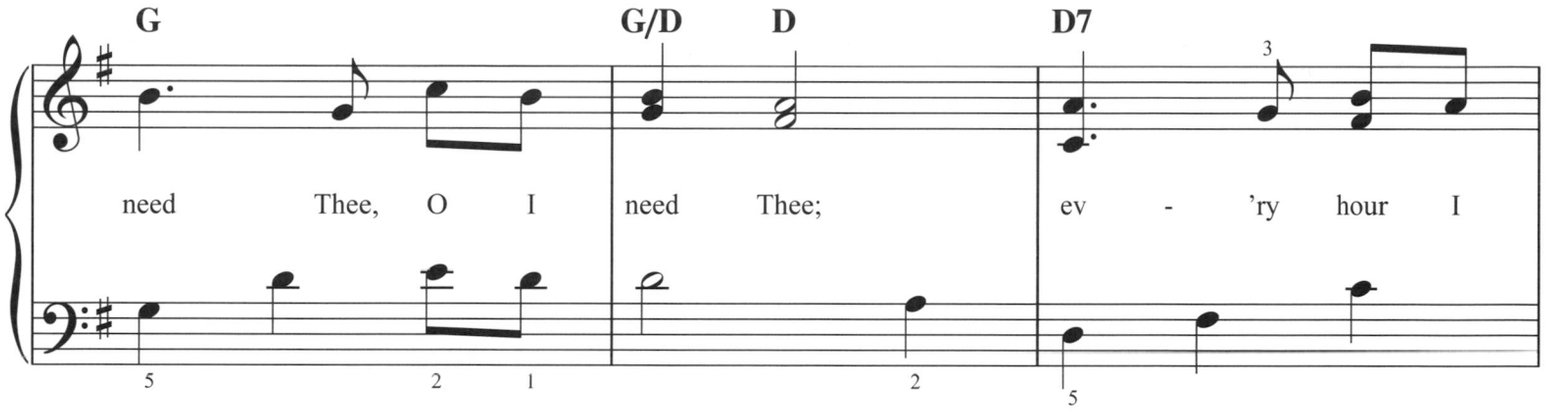
G
G/D
D
D7
need Thee, O I need Thee; ev - 'ry hour I

G
C
G
Cdim7/E♭
need Thee! O bless me now, my Sav - ior; I

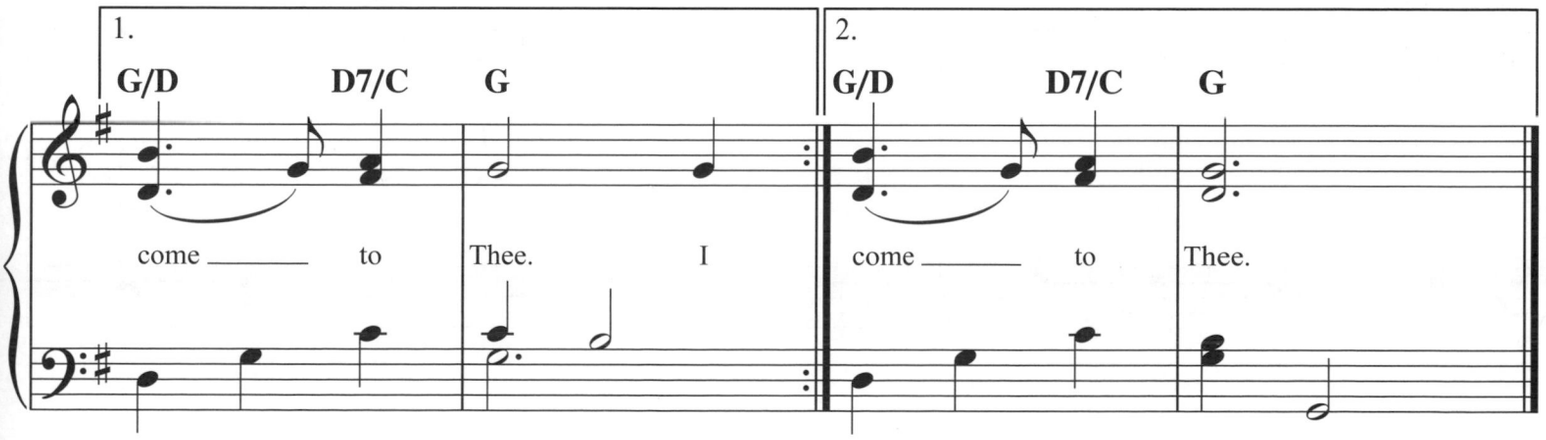
1.
G/D
D7/C
G
come to Thee. I
2.
G/D
D7/C
G
come to Thee.

# I SING THE MIGHTY POWER OF GOD

Words by ISAAC WATTS
Music from *Gesangbuch der Herzogl*

Copyright © 2018 by HAL LEONARD LLC
International Copyright Secured All Rights Reserved

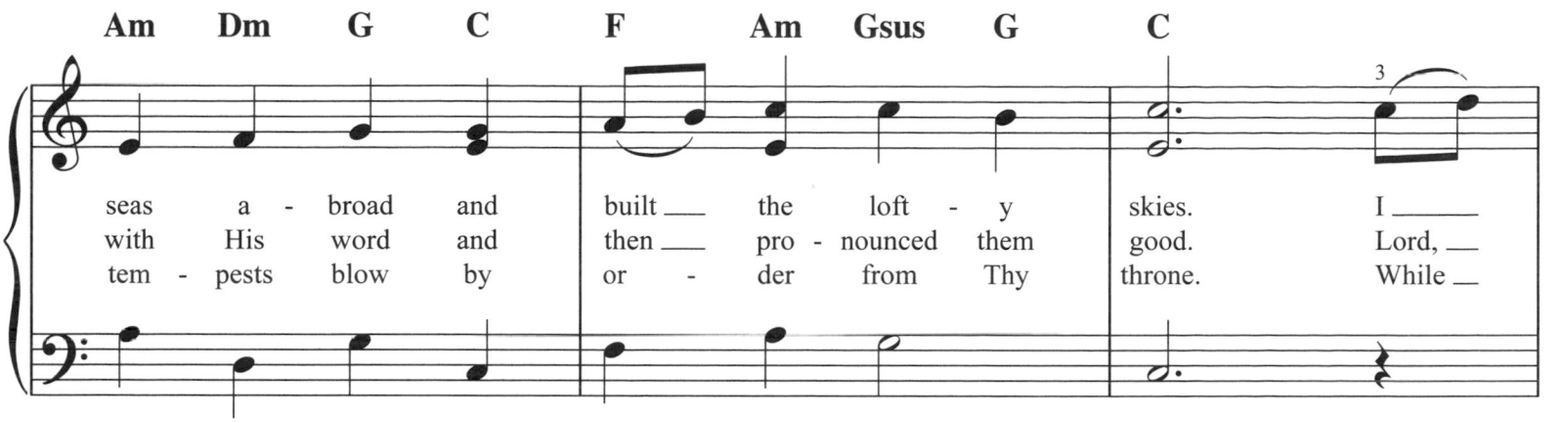
Am Dm G C F Am Gsus G C
seas a - broad and built the loft - y skies. I
with His word and then pro - nounced them good. Lord,
tem - pests blow by or - der from Thy throne. While

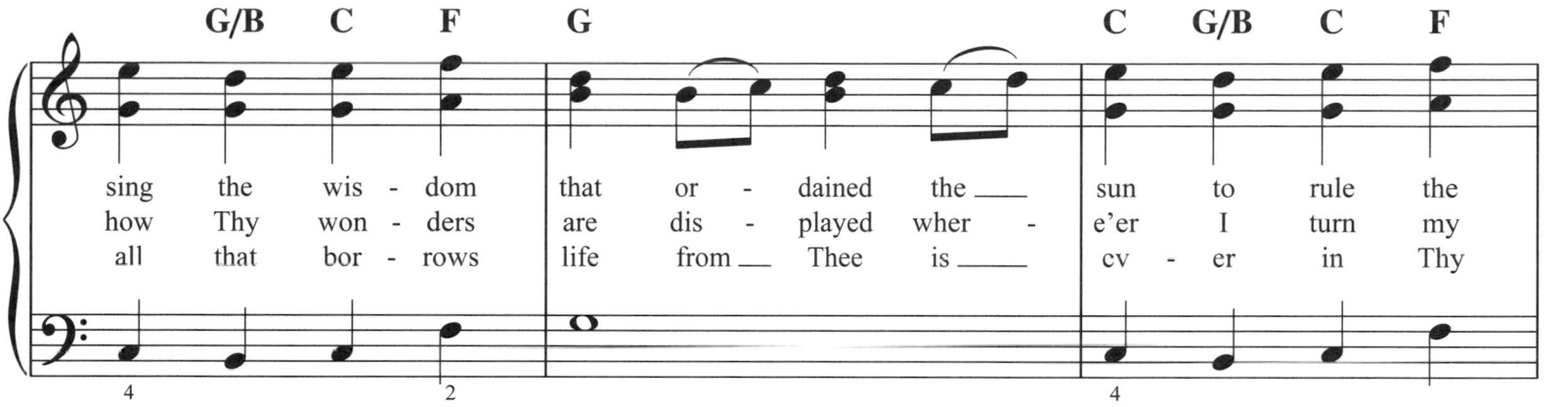
G/B C F G C G/B C F
sing the wis - dom that or - dained the sun to rule the
how Thy won - ders are dis - played wher - e'er I turn my
all that bor - rows life from Thee is ev - er in Thy

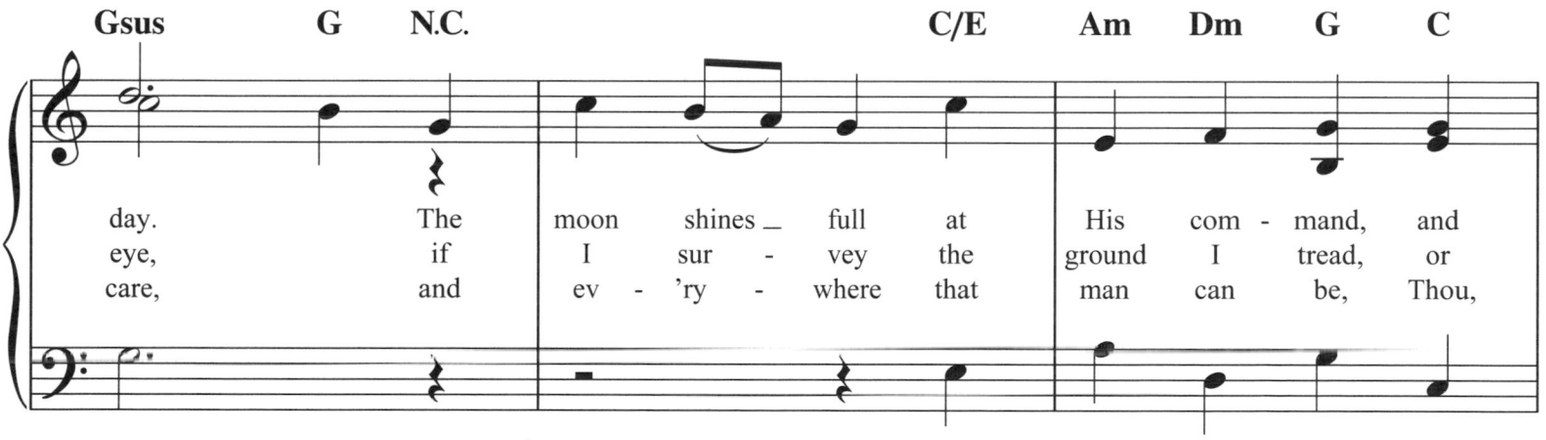
Gsus G N.C. C/E Am Dm G C
day. The moon shines full at His com - mand, and
eye, if I sur - vey the ground I tread, or
care, and ev - 'ry - where that man can be, Thou,

F Am Gsus G
1., 2. Csus C
3. Csus C
all the stars o - bey. I
gaze up - on the sky! There's
God, art pres - ent there.

# I SURRENDER ALL

Words by J.W. VAN DEVENTER
Music by W.S. WEEDEN

Copyright © 2018 by HAL LEONARD LLC
International Copyright Secured All Rights Reserved

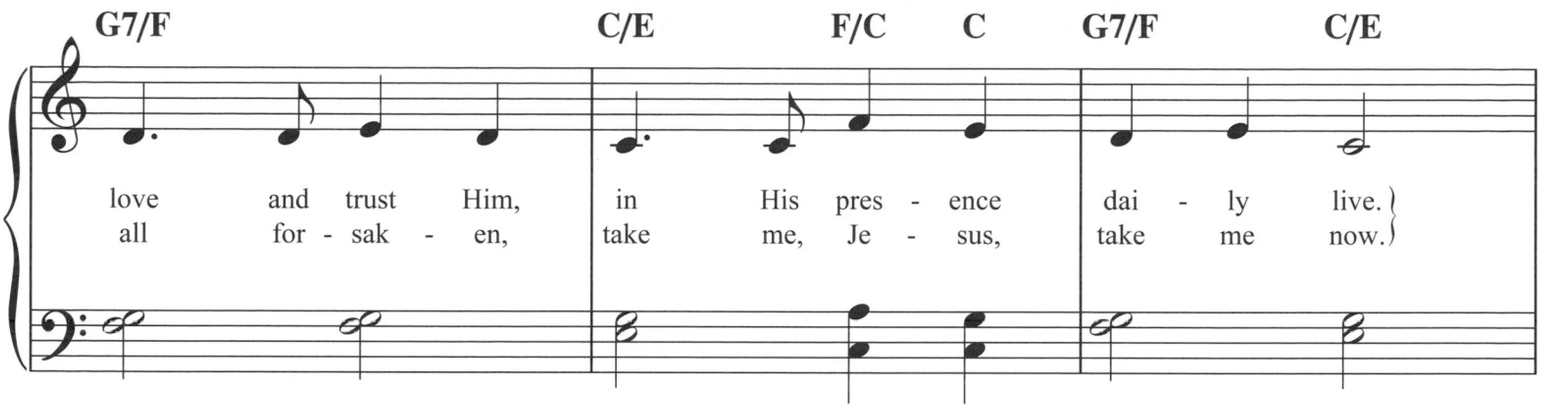
G7/F C/E F/C C G7/F C/E
love and trust Him, in His pres - ence dai - ly live.
all for - sak - en, take me, Je - sus, take me now.

C G7
I sur - ren - der all, I sur - ren - der
5

C F/C C F
all. All to Thee, my bless - ed Sav - ior,
5

C/G G
1. C
2. C
I sur - ren - der all. all.

# IMMORTAL, INVISIBLE

Words by WALTER CHALMERS SMITH
Traditional Welsh Melody
From John Roberts' *Canaidau y Cyssegr*

Copyright © 2018 by HAL LEONARD LLC
International Copyright Secured All Rights Reserved

D Em G/D D7/C G
ces - si - ble hid from our eyes, most
wast - ing, Thou rul - est in might; Thy
liv - est, the true life of all; we
Em D/F♯ G G/B
bless - ed, most glo - rious, the An - cient of
jus - tice like moun - tains high soar - ing a -
blos - som and flour - ish as leaves on the
Dsus D C Am D Em
Days, Al - might - y, vic - to - rious Thy
bove Thy clouds which are foun - tains of
tree, and with - er and per - ish, but
1., 2.
3.
G/D D7/C G G G
great Name we praise. Un -
good - ness and love. To
naught chang - eth Thee.

# IT IS WELL WITH MY SOUL

Words by HORATIO G. SPAFFORD
Music by PHILIP P. BLISS

Copyright © 2014 by HAL LEONARD CORPORATION
International Copyright Secured All Rights Reserved

G C E F D
roll; what - ev - er my lot, Thou hast taught me to
trol, that Christ has re - gard - ed my help - less es -

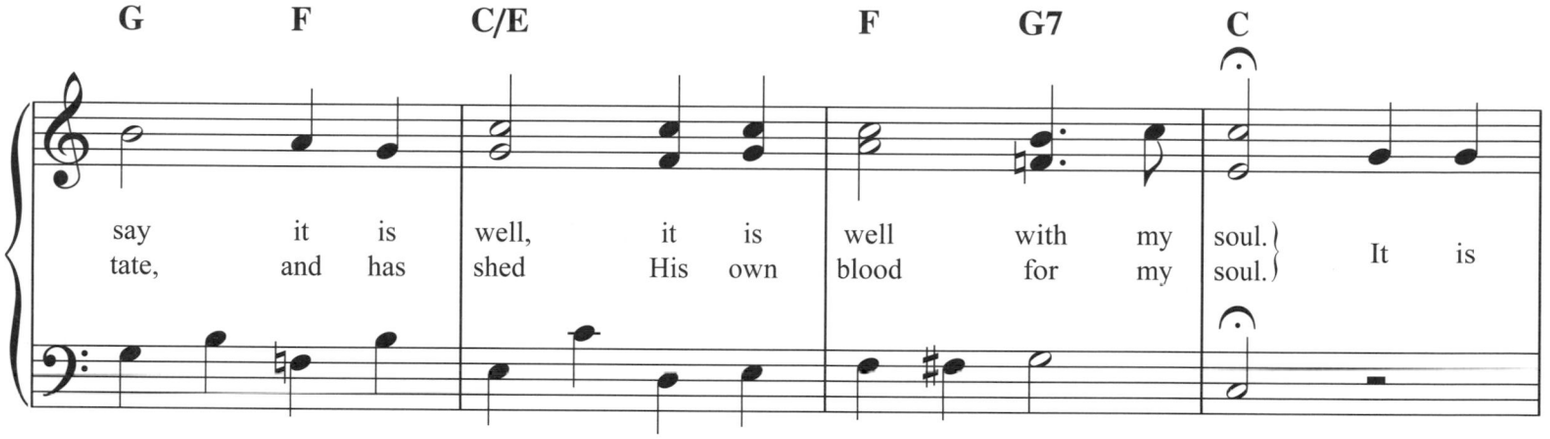
G F C/E F G7 C
say it is well, it is well with my soul.
tate, and has shed His own blood for my soul.
It is

G F G G♯dim Am C7
well (it is well) with my soul (with my soul). It is

F Dm7 G7 1. C 2. C
well, it is well with my soul. Though soul.

# JESUS PAID IT ALL

Words by ELVINA M. HALL
Music by JOHN T. GRAPE

Copyright © 2018 by HAL LEONARD LLC
International Copyright Secured All Rights Reserved

# NEARER, MY GOD, TO THEE

Words by SARAH F. ADAMS
Based on Genesis 28:10-22
Music by LOWELL MASON

Copyright © 1993 by HAL LEONARD CORPORATION
International Copyright Secured All Rights Reserved

# JESUS SHALL REIGN

Words by ISAAC WATTS
Music by JOHN HATTON

Copyright © 2018 by HAL LEONARD LLC
International Copyright Secured All Rights Reserved

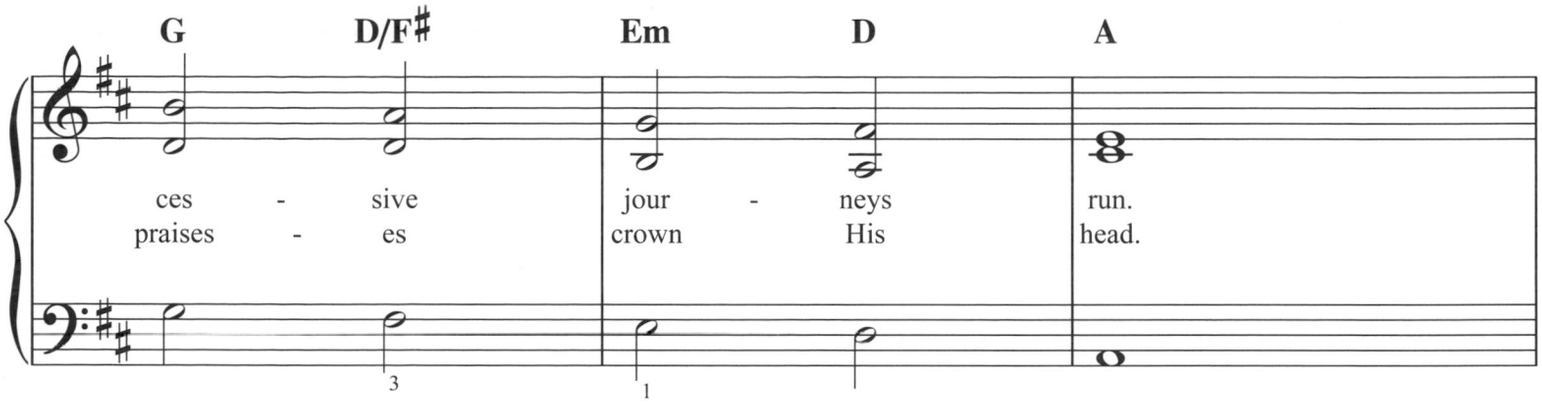
G D/F♯ Em D A
ces - sive jour - neys run.
praises - es crown His head.

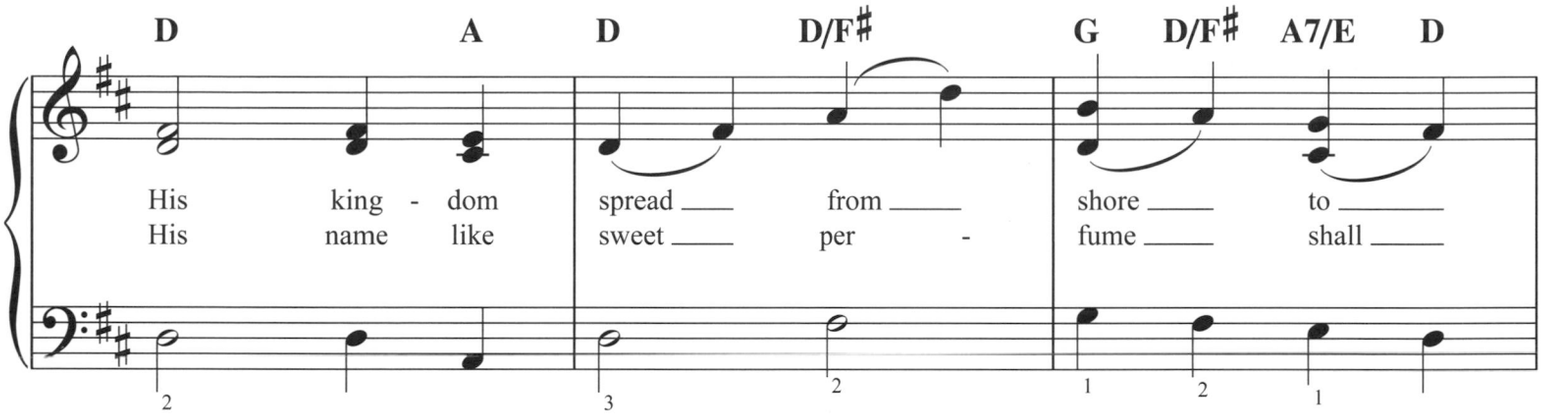
D A D D/F♯ G D/F♯ A7/E D
His king - dom spread ___ from ___ shore ___ to ___
His name like sweet ___ per - fume ___ shall ___

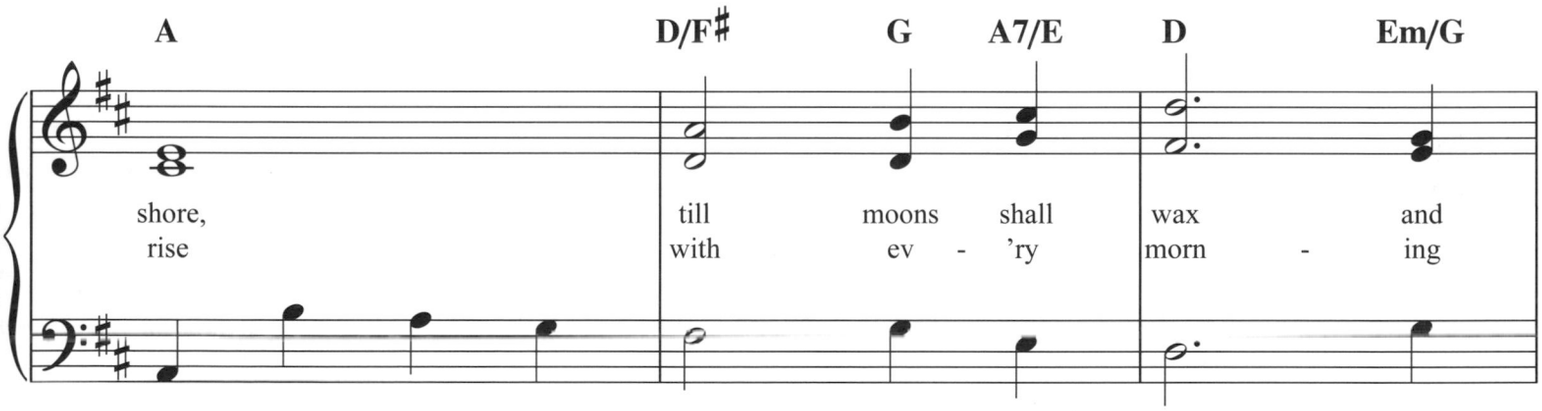
A D/F♯ G A7/E D Em/G
shore, till moons shall wax and
rise with ev - 'ry morn - ing

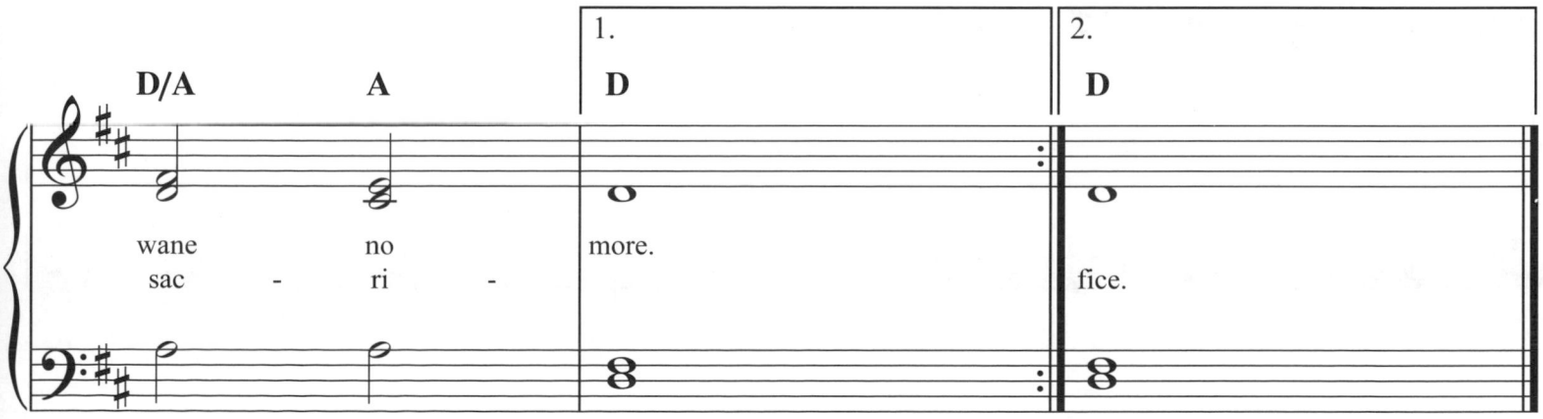
1.
2.
D/A A D D
wane no more.
sac - ri - fice.

# JOYFUL, JOYFUL, WE ADORE THEE

Words by HENRY VAN DYKE
Music by LUDWIG VAN BEETHOVEN,
melody from *Ninth Symphony*
Adapted by EDWARD HODGES

Copyright © 2004 by HAL LEONARD CORPORATION
International Copyright Secured All Rights Reserved

C G/D D7 G
flow'rs be - fore Thee, o - p'ning to the sun a - bove.
sing a - round Thee, cen - ter of un - bro - ken praise.
D G/D D G/D D B/D♯
Melt the clouds of sin and sad - ness, drive the dark of
Field and for - est, vale and moun - tain, flow - 'ry mead - ow,
Em A D G C/G G7 C
doubt a - way; Giv - er of im - mor - tal glad - ness,
flash - ing sea, chant - ing bird and flow - ing foun - tain
G/D
fill us with the
call us to re -
1.
D7 G
light of day.
2.
D7 G
joice in Thee.

# LEANING ON THE EVERLASTING ARMS

Words by ELISHA A. HOFFMAN
Music by ANTHONY J. SHOWALTER

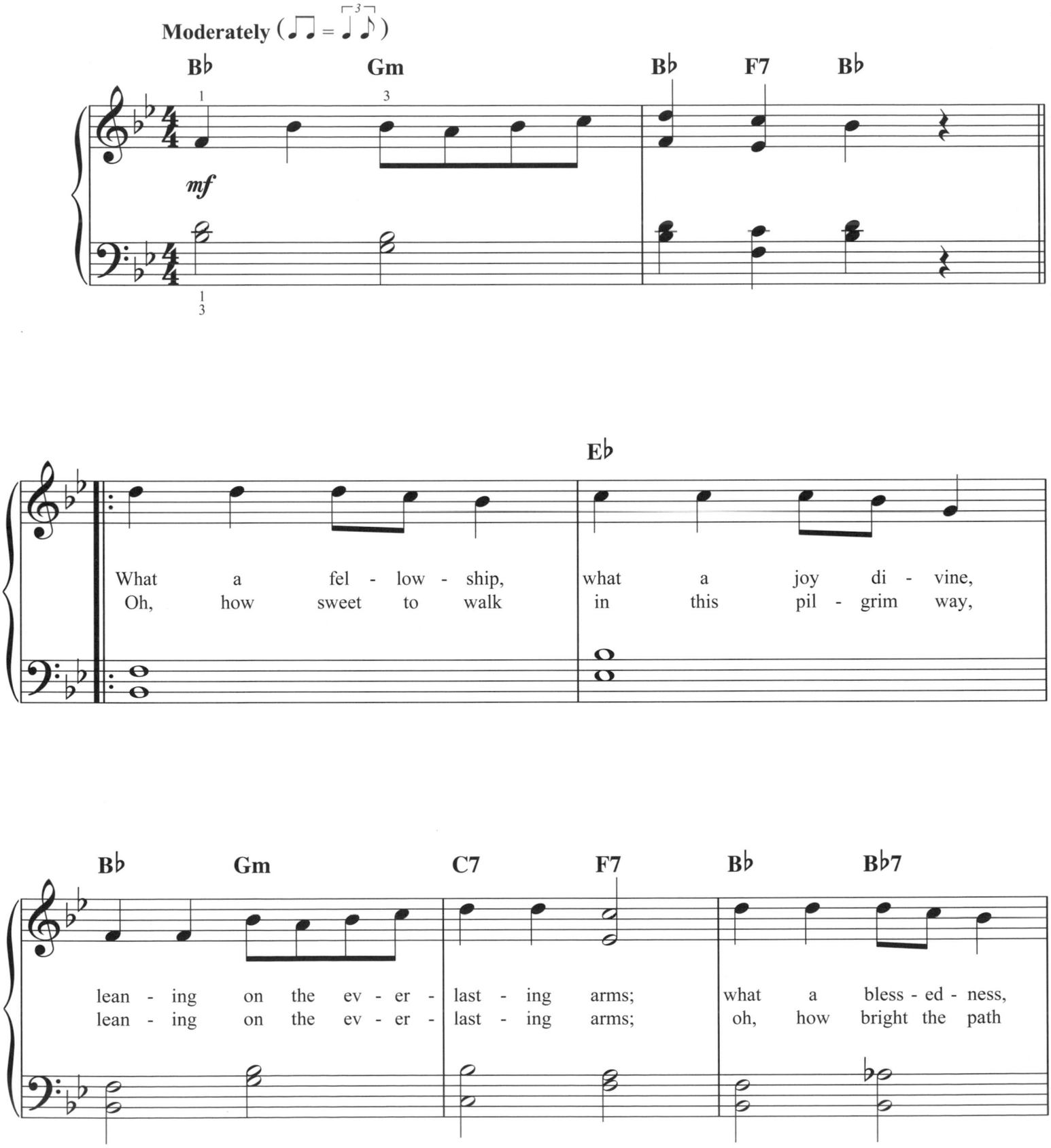


Copyright © 2018 by HAL LEONARD LLC
International Copyright Secured All Rights Reserved

E♭ B♭ Gm B♭/F F7 B♭
what a peace is mine, lean - ing on the ev - er - last - ing arms.
grows from day to day, lean - ing on the ev - er - last - ing arms.
E♭ B♭
Lean - ing, lean - ing, safe and se - cure from
C7 F7 B♭ B♭7 E♭
all a - larms; lean - ing, lean - ing,
B♭/F Gm
1. B♭/F F7 B♭
2. B♭/F F7 B♭
lean - ing on the ev - er - last - ing arms. last - ing arms.

# A MIGHTY FORTRESS IS OUR GOD

Words and Music by MARTIN LUTHER
Translated by FREDERICK H. HEDGE
Based on Psalm 46

Copyright © 2014 by HAL LEONARD CORPORATION
International Copyright Secured All Rights Reserved

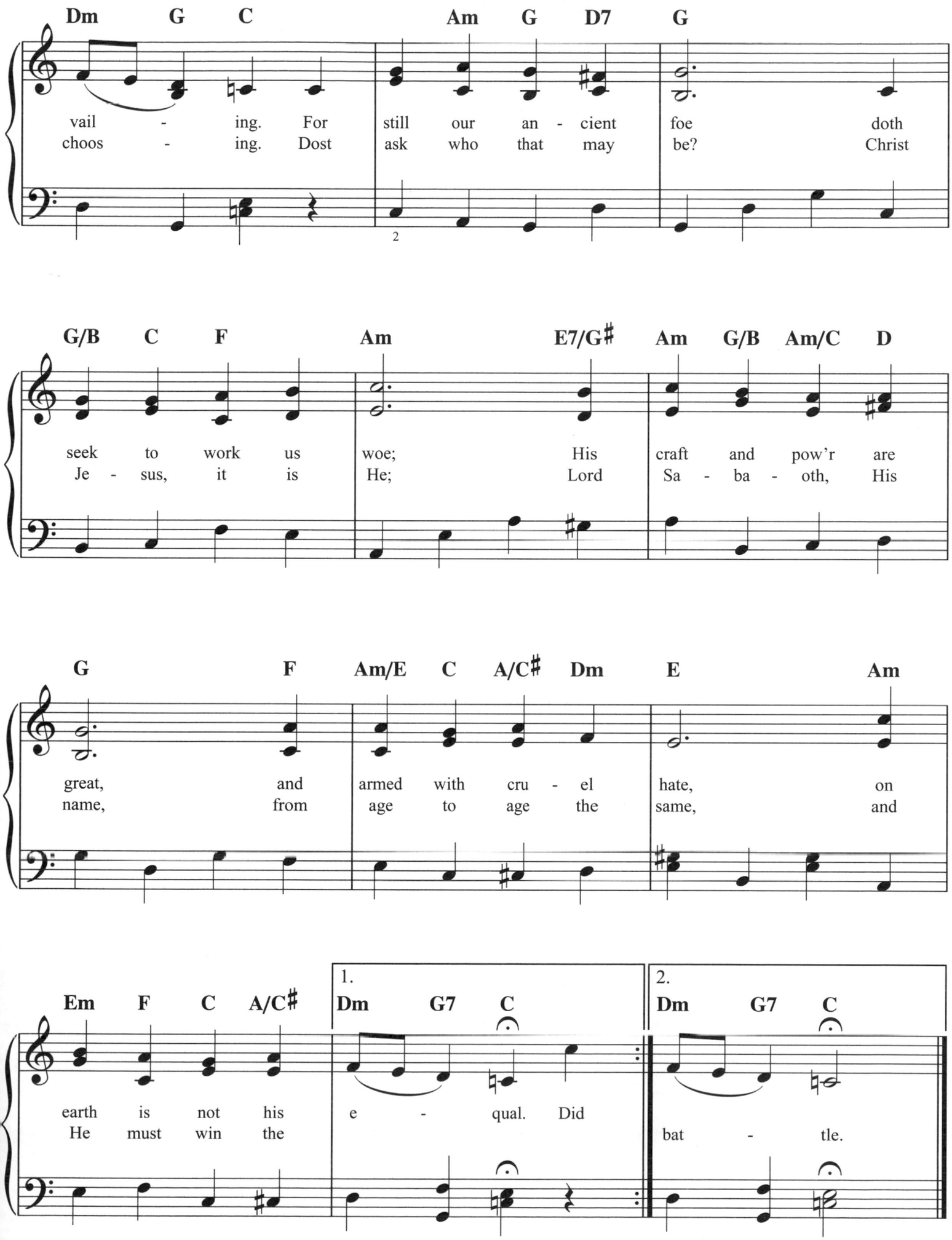
Dm G C Am G D7 G
vail - ing. For still our an - cient foe doth
choos - ing. Dost ask who that may be? Christ
2
G/B C F Am E7/G♯ Am G/B Am/C D
seek to work us woe; His craft and pow'r are
Je - sus, it is He; Lord Sa - ba - oth, His
G F Am/E C A/C♯ Dm E Am
great, and armed with cru - el hate, on
name, from age to age the same, and
Em F C A/C♯
earth is not his
He must win the
1.
Dm G7 C
e - qual. Did
2.
Dm G7 C
bat - tle.

# MY FAITH LOOKS UP TO THEE

Words by RAY PALMER
Music by LOWELL MASON

Copyright © 2004 by HAL LEONARD CORPORATION
International Copyright Secured All Rights Reserved

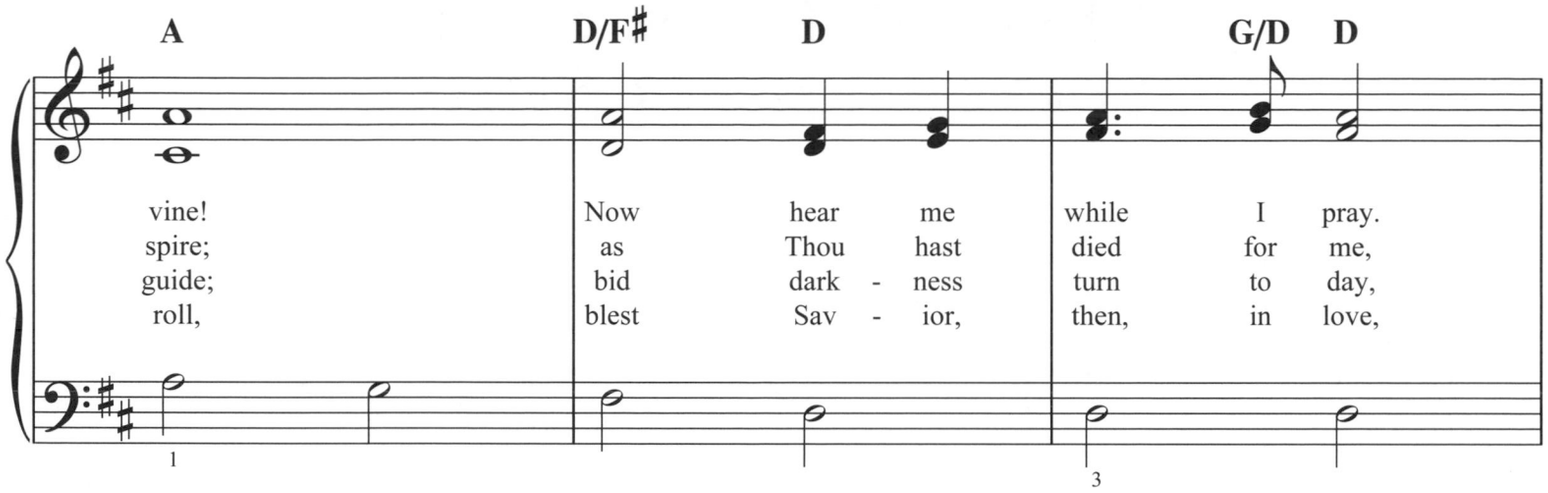
A D/F♯ D G/D D
vine! Now hear me while I pray.
spire; as Thou hast died for me,
guide; bid dark - ness turn to day,
roll, blest Sav - ior, then, in love,
1
3

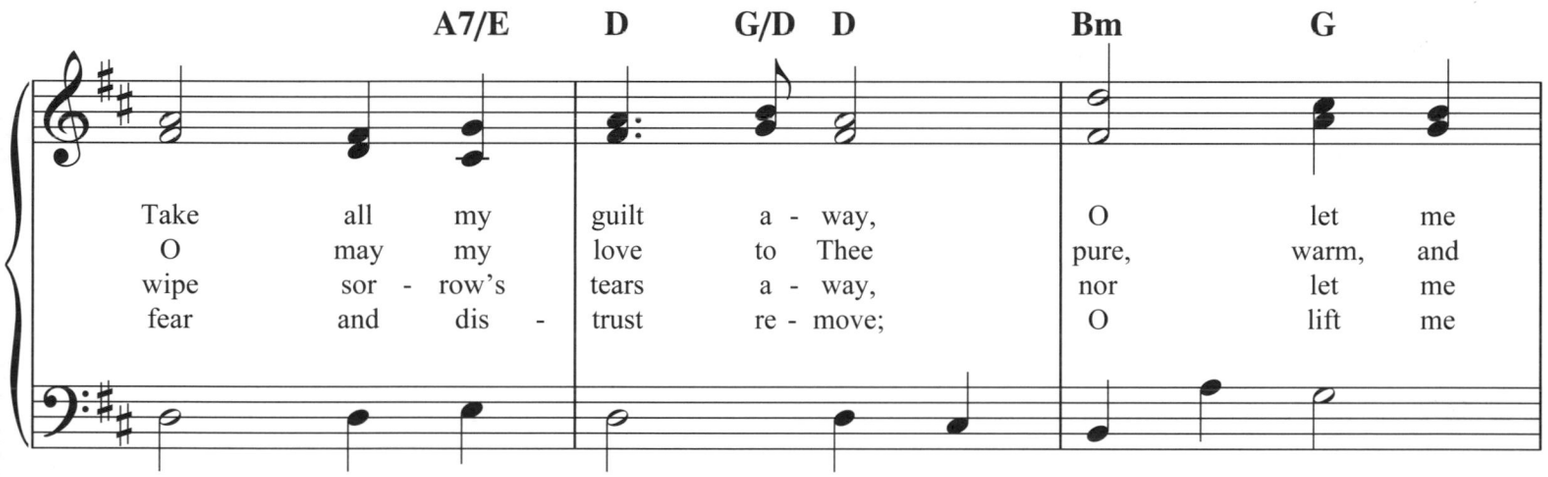
A7/E D G/D D Bm G
Take all my guilt a - way, O let me
O may my love to Thee pure, warm, and
wipe sor - row's tears a - way, nor let me
fear and dis - trust re - move; O lift me

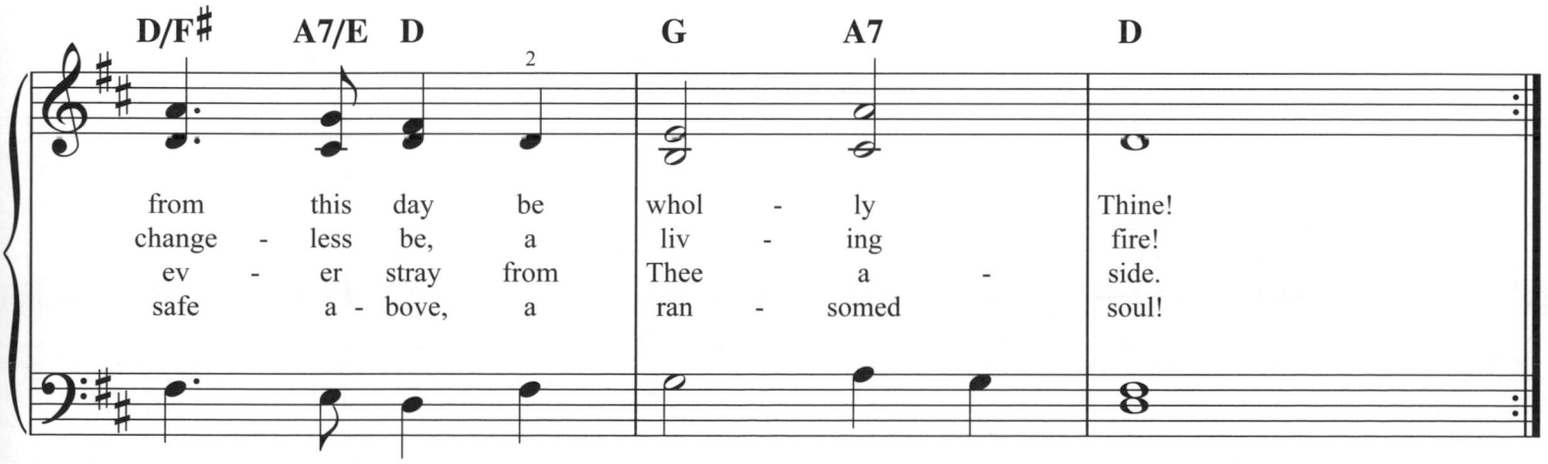
D/F♯ A7/E D G A7 D
2
from this day be whol - ly Thine!
change - less be, a liv - ing fire!
ev - er stray from Thee a - side.
safe a - bove, a ran - somed soul!

# O FOR A THOUSAND TONGUES TO SING

Words by CHARLES WESLEY
Music by CARL G. GLASER
Arranged by LOWELL MASON

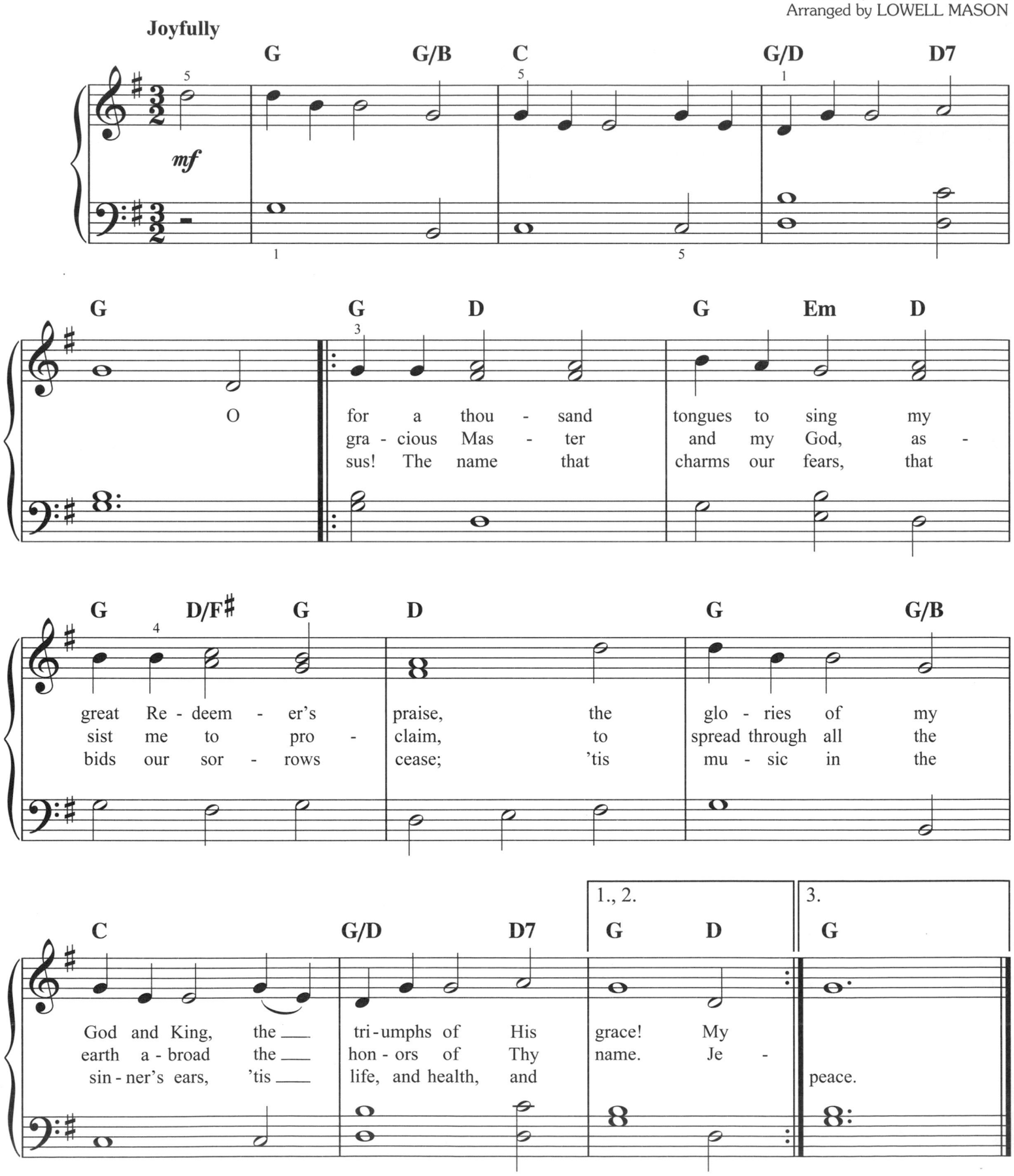


Copyright © 2018 by HAL LEONARD LLC
International Copyright Secured All Rights Reserved

# PRAISE GOD, FROM WHOM ALL BLESSINGS FLOW

Words by THOMAS KEN
Music Attributed to LOUIS BOURGEOIS

Copyright © 2018 by HAL LEONARD LLC
International Copyright Secured All Rights Reserved

# O MASTER, LET ME WALK WITH THEE

Words by WASHINGTON GLADDEN
Music by H. PERCY SMITH

Copyright © 2004 by HAL LEONARD CORPORATION
International Copyright Secured All Rights Reserved

Em7 D7/F♯ G Em A7
in low - ly paths of serv - ice
by some clear win - ning word of
in clos - er, dear - er com - pa -
D D/C G/B
free; tell me Thy se - cret,
love. Teach me the way - ward
ny, in work that keeps faith
C G/B Dsus D G D Em
help me bear the strain of
feet to stay, and guide them
sweet and strong, in trust that
D7/F♯ G C D G
toil, the fret of care.
in the home - ward way.
tri - umphs o - ver wrong.

# O WORSHIP THE KING

Words by ROBERT GRANT
Music attributed to JOHANN MICHAEL HAYDN
Arranged by WILLIAM GARDINER

Copyright © 2018 by HAL LEONARD LLC
International Copyright Secured All Rights Reserved

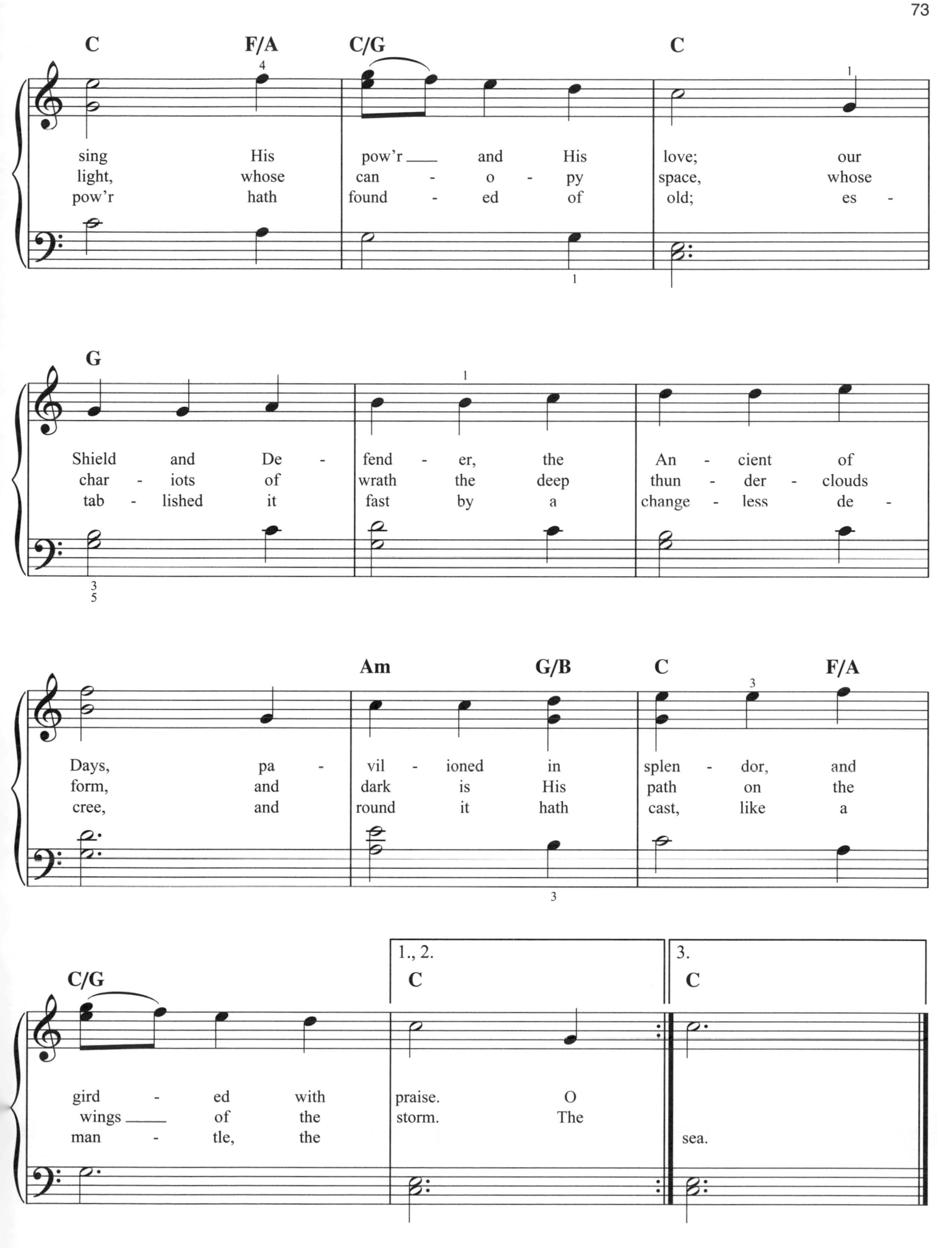
C F/A C/G C
sing His pow'r and His love; our
light, whose can - o - py space, whose
pow'r hath found - ed of old; es -
G
Shield and De - fend - er, the An - cient of
char - iots of wrath the deep thun - der - clouds
tab - lished it fast by a change - less de -
Am G/B C F/A
Days, pa - vil - ioned in splen - dor, and
form, and dark is His path on the
cree, and round it hath cast, like a
C/G
gird - ed with praise. O
wings of the storm. The
man - tle, the sea.
1., 2.
C
3.
C

# PRAISE TO THE LORD, THE ALMIGHTY

Words by JOACHIM NEANDER
Translated by CATHERINE WINKWORTH
Music from *Erneuerten Gesangbuch*

Copyright © 2018 by HAL LEONARD LLC
International Copyright Secured All Rights Reserved

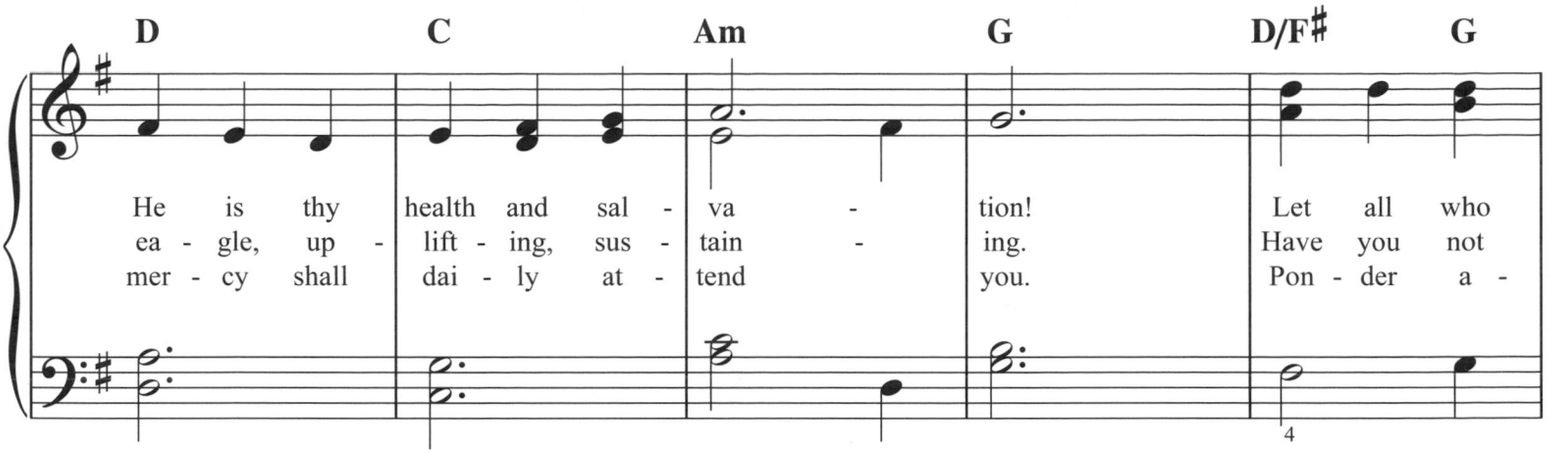
D C Am G D/F♯ G
He is thy health and sal - va - tion! Let all who
ea - gle, up - lift - ing, sus - tain - ing. Have you not
mer - cy shall dai - ly at - tend you. Pon - der a -
4

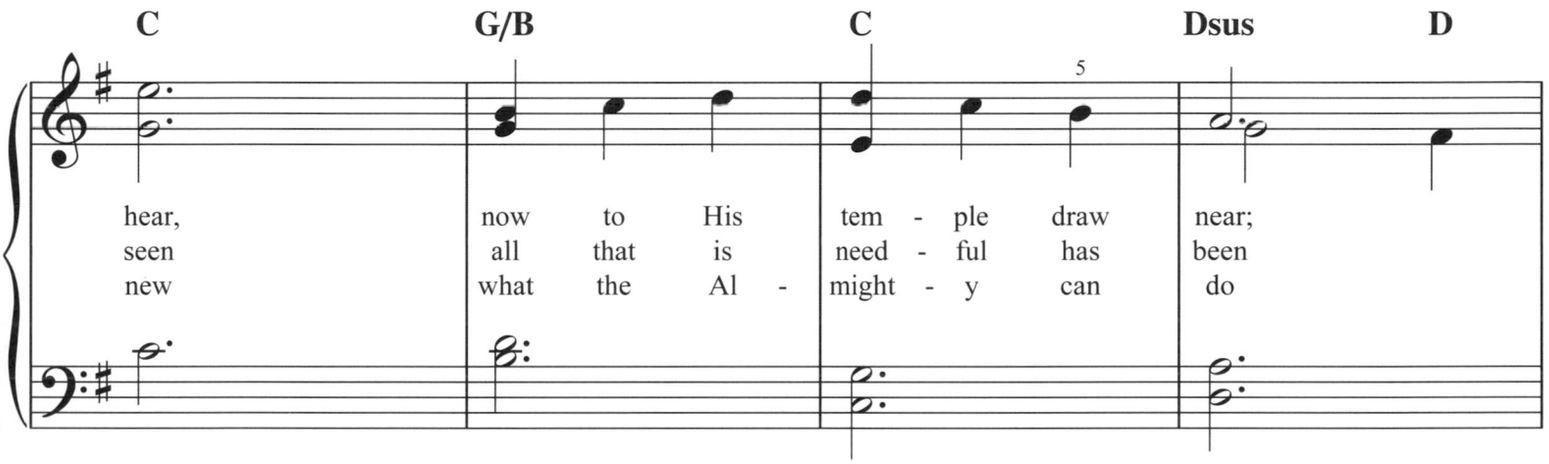
C G/B C Dsus D
5
hear, now to His tem - ple draw near;
seen all that is need - ful has been
new what the Al - might - y can do

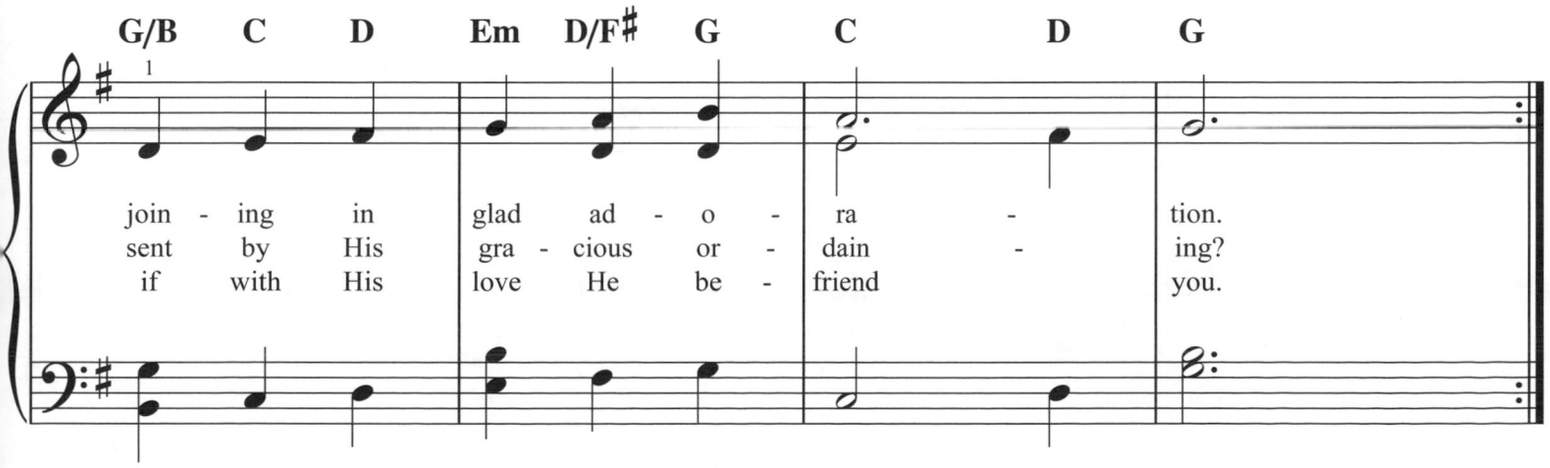
G/B C D Em D/F♯ G C D G
1
join - ing in glad ad - o - ra - tion.
sent by His gra - cious or - dain - ing?
if with His love He be - friend you.

# ROCK OF AGES

Words by AUGUSTUS M. TOPLADY
V.1,2,4 altered by THOMAS COTTERILL
Music by THOMAS HASTINGS

Copyright © 2018 by HAL LEONARD LLC
International Copyright Secured All Rights Reserved

# SOFTLY AND TENDERLY

Words and Music by
WILL L. THOMPSON

Copyright © 2018 by HAL LEONARD LLC
International Copyright Secured All Rights Reserved

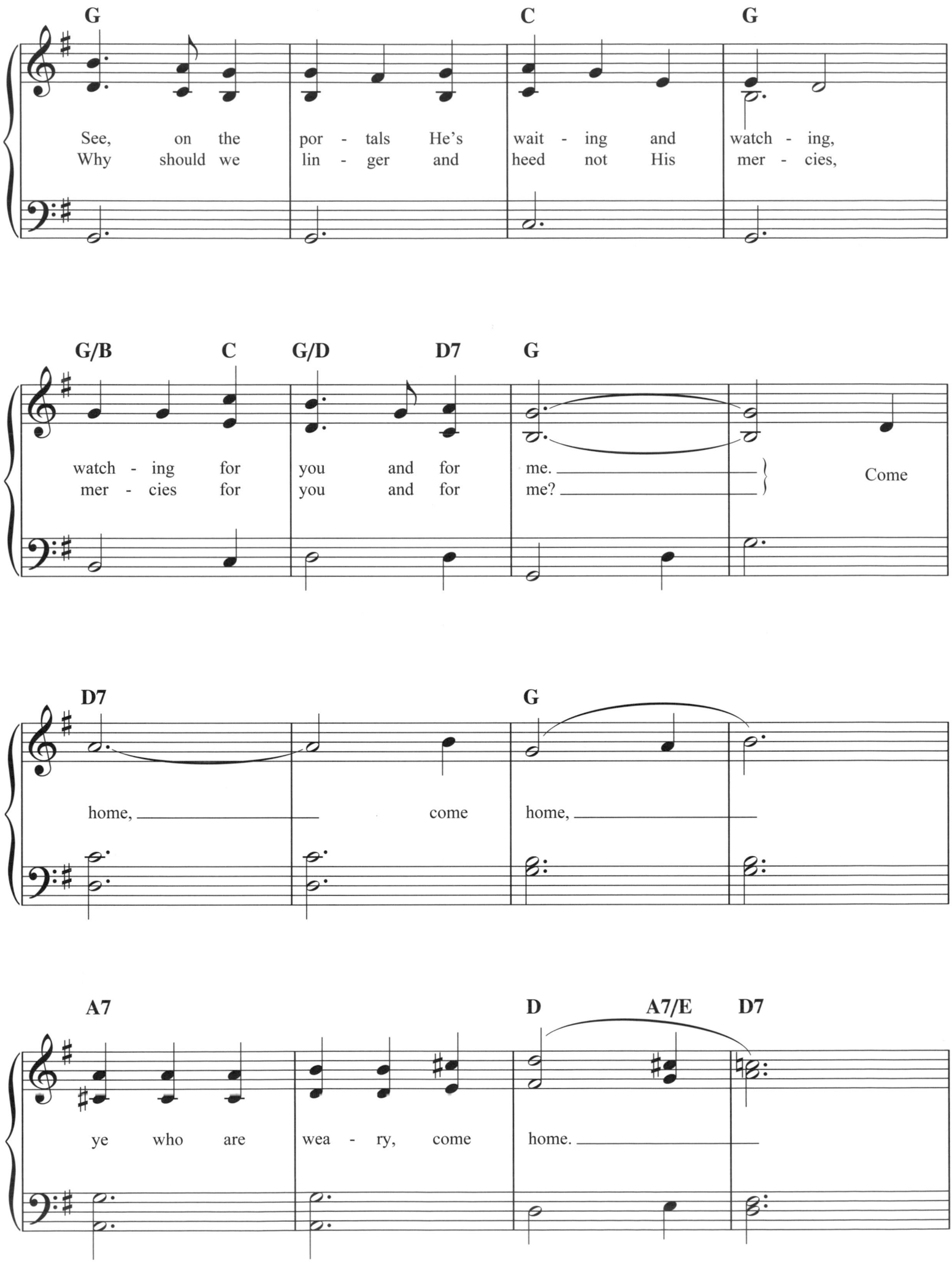
G C G
See, on the por - tals He's wait - ing and watch - ing,
Why should we lin - ger and heed not His mer - cies,
G/B C G/D D7 G
watch - ing for you and for me.
mer - cies for you and for me?
Come
D7 G
home, come home,
A7 D A7/E D7
ye who are wea - ry, come home.

G
C
G
Ear - nest - ly, ten - der - ly, Je - sus is call - ing,
G/B
C
G/D
D7
1.
G
D7
call - ing, O sin - ner, come home!
2.
G
Am7
home!
G
Am7
G

# SAVIOR, LIKE A SHEPHERD LEAD US

Words from *Hymns For The Young*
Attributed to DOROTHY A. THRUPP
Music by WILLIAM B. BRADBURY

Copyright © 2018 by HAL LEONARD LLC
International Copyright Secured All Rights Reserved

Dm Gm7 C7 F F7/A
feed ___ us, ___ for our use Thy folds pre - pare. Bless - ed
fend ___ us, ___ seek us when we go a - stray. Bless - ed
B♭ Bdim7 F/C Dm Gm7 C7
Je - sus, Bless - ed Je - sus, Thou hast bought us, Thine we
Je - sus, Bless - ed Je - sus, hear, O hear us when we
F F7/A B♭ Bdim7 F/C Dm
are; Bless - ed Je - sus, Bless - ed Je - sus, Thou hast
pray; Bless - ed Je - sus, Bless - ed Je - sus, hear, O
Gm7 C7 1. B♭ F 2. B♭ F
bought us, Thine we are.
hear us when we pray.

# THIS IS MY FATHER'S WORLD

Words by MALTBIE D. BABCOCK
Music by FRANKLIN L. SHEPPARD

Copyright © 2018 by HAL LEONARD LLC
International Copyright Secured All Rights Reserved

A7/G D/F♯ A7/G D
round me rings the mu - sic of the ___ spheres. This
lil - y white, de - clare ___ their Mak - er's ___ praise. This
oft so strong, God is ___ the rul - er ___ yet. This
G A/E D G/D D G/D
is my Fa - ther's world: I ___ rest me in the
is my Fa - ther's world: He ___ shines in all that's
is my Fa - ther's world: why ___ should my heart be
D A7 D A7/G D/F♯
thought of rocks and trees, of ___ skies and seas; His
fair; in the rust - ling grass I ___ hear Him pass; He
sad? The Lord is King; let ___ heav - ens ring! God
1., 2. 3.
D A7/G D D
hand ___ the won - ders ___ wrought. This ___
speaks ___ to me ev - 'ry - where. This ___
reigns; ___ let the earth be ___ glad!

# 'TIS SO SWEET TO TRUST IN JESUS

Words by LOUISA M.R. STEAD
Music by WILLIAM J. KIRKPATRICK

Copyright © 2018 by HAL LEONARD LLC
International Copyright Secured All Rights Reserved

C C/G G C G/D G
on His prom - ise, just to know "Thus saith the Lord."
faith to plunge me 'neath the heal - ing, cleans - ing flood!
D G
Je - sus, Je - sus, how I trust Him! How I've proved Him
D A7 D G C C/G G
o'er and o'er! Je - sus, Je - sus, pre - cious Je - sus!
C
O for grace to
1., 2.
G/D D G
trust Him more!
3.
G/D D G
trust Him more!

# WE GATHER TOGETHER

Words from *Nederlandtsch Gedenckclanck*
Translated by THEODORE BAKER
Netherlands Folk Melody
Arranged by EDWARD KREMSER

Copyright © 2018 by HAL LEONARD LLC
International Copyright Secured All Rights Reserved

Am7 G/B Am/C D G
has - tens His will to make known. The
tain - ing His king - dom di - vine. So
still our De - fend - er will be. Let
G/F C/E Dm7 G7
wick - ed op - press - ing now cease from dis -
from the be - gin - ning the fight we were
Thy con - gre - ga - tion es - cape trib - u -
C F C
tress - ing. Sing prais - es to His name; He for -
win - ning. Thou, Lord, was at our side; all
la - tion. Thy name be ev - er praised! O
G7 1., 2. C 3. C
gets not His own. Be -
glo - ry be Thine! We
Lord, make us free!

# WERE YOU THERE?

Traditional Spiritual
Harmony by CHARLES WINFRED DOUGLAS

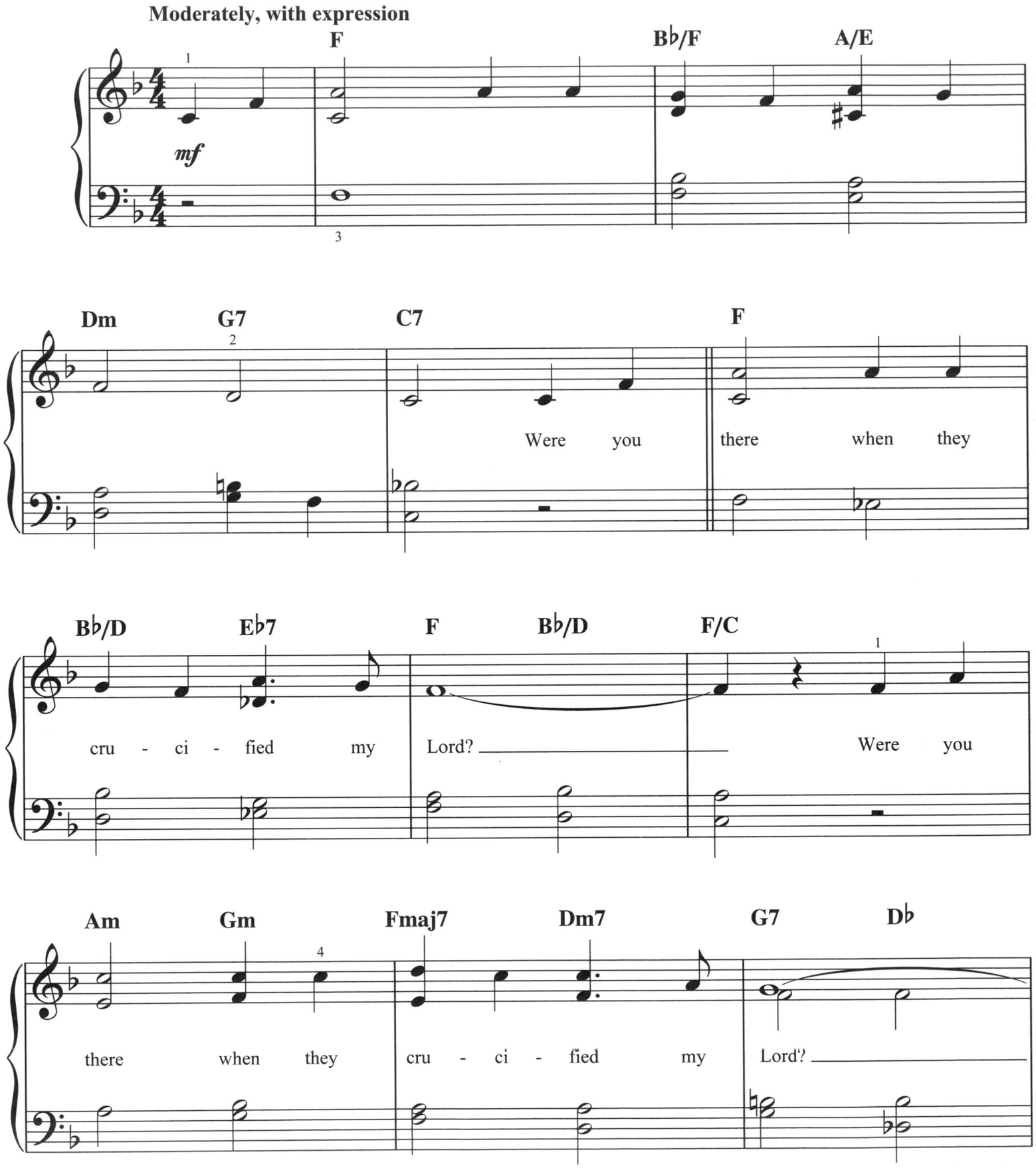


Copyright © 2018 by HAL LEONARD LLC
International Copyright Secured All Rights Reserved

C7 F B♭/D Cm7 F
Oh!
B♭ F7 A/C♯ Dm B♭
Some - times it cause - es me to trem - ble,
D♭ C7 C7sus E♭7 F B7
trem - ble, trem - ble. Were you there when they
B♭ C7 F B♭7/A♭ F
cru - ci - fied my Lord?

# WHAT A FRIEND WE HAVE IN JESUS

Words by JOSEPH M. SCRIVEN
Music by CHARLES C. CONVERSE

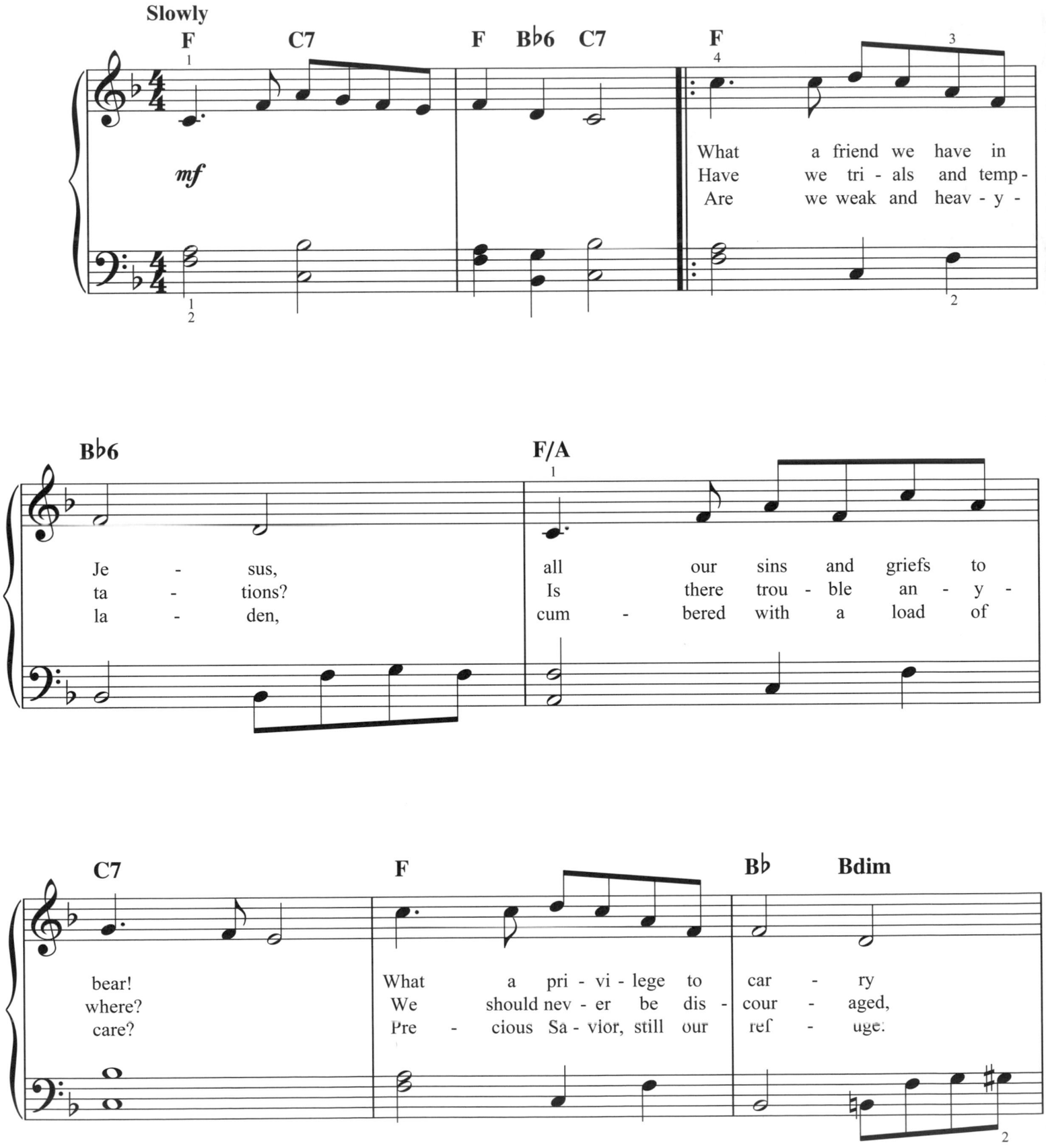


Copyright © 2018 by HAL LEONARD LLC
International Copyright Secured All Rights Reserved

F/C C7 F B♭7 F C7
ev - 'ry - thing to God in prayer! Oh, what peace we of - ten
take it to the Lord in prayer! Can we find a friend so
take it to the Lord in prayer. Do thy friends de - spise, for -
F B♭ F/A C
for - feit, oh, what need - less pain we bear,
faith - ful, who will all our sor - rows share?
sake thee? Take it to the Lord in prayer.
F B♭ Bdim
all be - cause we do not car - ry
Je - sus knows our ev - 'ry weak - ness,
In His arms He'll take and shield thee;
F/C C7
ev - 'ry - thing to God in
take it to the Lord in
thou will find a so - lace
1., 2.
F B♭6 C7
prayer.
prayer.
3.
F B♭6 F
there.
rit.

# WHITER THAN SNOW

Words by JAMES L. NICHOLSON
Music by WILLIAM G. FISCHER

Copyright © 2018 by HAL LEONARD LLC
International Copyright Secured All Rights Reserved

C/G
C
G
i - dol, cast out ev - 'ry foe; now wash me and
self, and what - ev - er I know, now wash me and
D7
G
D
I shall be whit - er than snow.
I shall be whit - er than snow.
Whit - er than
D7
Em
C
G
C
snow, yes, whit - er than snow, now wash me, and
G
D7
1.
G
2.
G
I shall be whit - er than snow. Lord snow.

# WONDROUS LOVE

Southern American Folk Hymn

Copyright © 2018 by HAL LEONARD LLC
International Copyright Secured All Rights Reserved

Dm C Dm F Dm F Am
___ What won - drous love is this that caused the Lord _ of
___ To God and to the Lamb who is the great _ I
___ And when from death I'm free I'll sing and joy - ful
Dm Am Dm C
bliss to bear the dread - ful curse for my
Am, while mil - lions join the theme, I will
be, and through e - ter - ni - ty I'll sing
Dm Am Dm F Am Dm C
soul, for my soul, to bear the dread - ful curse for my
sing, I will sing, while mil - lions join the theme I will
on, I'll sing on, and through e - ter - ni - ty I'll sing
1., 2.
Dm Gm/D Dm
soul. ___ When
sing. ___ And
3.
Dm Gm/D Dm
on. ___

# WHEN I SURVEY THE WONDROUS CROSS

Words by ISAAC WATTS
Music arranged by LOWELL MASON
Based on Plainsong

Copyright © 2018 by HAL LEONARD LLC
International Copyright Secured All Rights Reserved